REVIEWS BY READERS

Shirley Barasch's memoir *For Professional Purposes, an artistic journey*, invites the reader on a visual and sensory journey of discovery, awakening, mischief, loss and triumph of a gifted, determined girl through the depression and World War II years in Pittsburgh, Pennsylvania. We meet unforgettable characters along the way through the Squirrel Hill section—bakeries, synagogues, businesses, schools, and the trolleys, and well, back yards she shortcuts through and even Kennywood Park in vivid details. The trip will be at once nostalgic and fresh as we travel along with that child on a heart stopping adventure of a budding artist coming of age. All readers as well as those familiar with Dr. Barasch's distinguished career will be surprised and impressed to know her beginnings.

Tikvah Feinstein, Journalist and Editor/publisher *Taproot Literary Review*. Author of *Inanna, Tiamat: A Prehistoric Adventure More True Than Fiction, Music From a Broken Violin*

Beautiful, evocative and heartwarming...sensory detail is excellent. I was right there in her childhood world...loved the family recipes.

Kathy Bashaar, Moderator, Pleasant Hills Library, PA Writing Group

For Professional Purposes is a charming coming of age tale set in Pittsburgh. Our little Shirley will charm you all the way through. You'll cheer at her triumphs and be devastated by her adversities. But whatever you're feeling, this emotional roller coaster will give you a ride you'll not soon forget. Her music is her strength. It makes her who she is. I felt that I was right there, by her side, every step of the way. I experienced what she experienced. Her joy was my joy. Her sorrow was my sorrow. This book is a "must read" for anyone with a heart.

Audrey Castracane, Actor/Director

You don't have to be Jewish to enjoy Shirley Barasch's *For Professional Purposes*, you don't have to be a woman, you don't even have to be from Pittsburgh! You just have to be a human being looking for a great read.

Richard Keitel, Professor of Theatre, Point Park University

This is a fascinating read. Suspenseful at times, surprisingly humorous, and frequently touching, it is filled with keenly observed and remembered details from a bygone era. This candid "portrait of the artist" as a young girl had me rooting for that little girl and marveling at her determination to blossom despite the odds against her. I thoroughly enjoyed it.

    Shirley Tannenbaum, Associate Professor of Theatre,

    Point Park University

Have your box of tissues ready as you read Shirley Barasch's *moving* coming-of-age story.

    Elizabeth Samet, Creative Director, Time Inc.

The original staged reading of Shirley Barasch's "For Professional Purposes: an artistic journey," featured local actors playing a noisy, combative immigrant Jewish family. Transformed into a memoir, it is a compelling first person narrative of the young girl—front and center—striving to realize her musical gifts. The story evoking the hardscrabble times and dissonant family, rings true. For extra measure the author enriches her sensual memories with a collection of family recipes mirroring the full life the women provided. This is a wonderfully satisfying treat of a book.

    E.P.Welling, Professional Copyreader/Editor

Passionately driven by her love of music and extraordinary talent, the author overcomes a difficult environment and family dynamic by not allowing anyone to stop her. I only hope that a second memoir will continue her story.

    Patricia Love Anouchi, Rehabilitation Counselor

Despite life's obstacles and hardships, our young heroine finds the courage to persevere through heartache and misery to find her voice. Very moving, indeed.

    Anne Beetem Barasch

ISBN: 146090348X
ISBN-13: 9781460903483
Library of Congress Control Number: 2011902058

FOR PROFESSIONAL PURPOSES

AN ARTISTIC JOURNEY

©2010

SHIRLEY R. BARASCH

A WORD FROM THE AUTHOR

This book originally began as three one acts written for the stage. It had one read through and a partially staged enactment. Everyone who played a role wanted me to take it further. Unfortunately, producing it on stage became overwhelming. Then I began adding to the story, taking down notes in a diary fashion. Discovering old report cards, letters and pictures made my past come alive. Touching base with former friends created a tidal wave of surprising recollections. Before I knew it, I had sketched a whole series of incidents and memories into twenty chapters about my life from age four to sixteen.

Then came my *eureka* moment! Food, cooking, and family eating had played a major part in my life and "boiled" over into the chapter titles of the memoir. It was then that I decided to include recipes of the fragrant memories of our family life around the table as part of the book along with family pictures. It took enormous effort to limit my collection to a handful for my memoir. What should I include that would be interesting to the reader that was not just my own sentimental choice?

Now you have it. The genesis of *For Professional Purposes, an artistic journey:* a young girl struggles to realize her own potential in a social order not yet ready for a woman to be an independent and creative person. Growing up, I never had an awareness of this process. I just lived it. Now as I look back, my life seems a story of survival through both lows and highs, and a bounty of rewards I am just beginning to appreciate.

Shirley R. Barasch

ACKNOWLEDGEMENTS

I will forever be grateful to those who encouraged me in putting this book together—and supported me as a writer, composer, and poet—but especially those early, gifted teachers: Mary Etta Allison, Laura Ziegler, Esther Long, T. Carl Whitmer, and Helene Welker, who saw in a young girl the seeds of what was possible.

Tikvah Feinstein—author of *Inanna of Tiamat: A Prehistoric Adventure More True than Fiction* and *Music from a Broken Violin*, journalist and editor/publisher of *Taproot Literary Review*, who published my poetry and kept me on track as a writer of this memoir and first recognized its publishing potential.

Elaine Pelaez Welling—whose ear for grammar and sense helped make the book a correct manuscript.

Ronald Louis Gigliotti—computer expert who made my old photos work.

Patty Goldberg Love Anouchi; Milton Wolf; Leona Podolsky Green; Marlene Blumenthal Landay Rebb; my cousin, Deanna Joy Lowe Sable—who helped me through good and tough times—and Cindy Ducsay, who read every word while we tested the recipes.

Barbara Lea Schiffman Samet—who lived through my experiences with me.

Larry Barasch, Karen Barasch Staif, and Miriam Barasch Fleming—my children who have shared, attended, and supported all my lifelong creative undertakings.

Ronald H. Barasch—my dear husband and best friend, who has always loyally applauded and patiently read as well as listened to any and all of my efforts. He spent many nights alone while I labored at the computer and keyboard. I could always count on his wonderful smile when I emerged from the depths of creative hell! To him I owe my stability and the freedom to be who I am.

And of course to all those at *CreateSpace*—who guided my book into print!

DEDICATION

This book is dedicated to my grandma, Mary Hofstadter Schiffman, who
made my survival possible.

Photo of Grandma dancing with Shirley Ruth Schiffman Barasch at
her wedding
August 15, 1954

For Professional Purposes
an artistic journey
1937–1949
by
Shirley R. Barasch

Chapter One

HAVDAHLAH AND HERRING
SEPTEMBER 1937

My new sister just got born. She doesn't look real new to me. Her legs are really squashed up and her hands are wrinkly and full of what Mommy says is dried skin. But what a flavor she is—just like vanilla ice cream when I'm 'lowed to kiss her real gentle. She has yellow fuzz on her head that Mommy says will be curls. But her eyes are wide open with some crumbs the sandman left in the corners. She looks at me even though Mommy says she can't see yet just like a baby kitten. I kin hardly wait to help feed her, but Daddy says I have to stay with Grandma for two weeks while Bubbie and Aunt Mayme help with the baby.

I want to take care of the baby. I'm already a big girl. I'm gonna be five. But Mommy says I can help right now if I bring her a white diaper and help her put it under the baby's chin. She shows me how she puts her brown nipple that squirts out blue-looking milk into Baby's little trembling mouth. I laugh 'cause some of the milk gets right on my fingers and I lick it quick and it tastes sweet and Mommy laughs, too.

"Is she gonna have a name?" I whisper.

"Barbara…Barbara Lea. Do you like that name?"

I nod and pat my little sister's head. Mommy kisses the baby's wrinkly hand, which is holding on to her finger so tight, and then she kisses my hand. Then I have to go with Daddy to stay with my Grandma in Squirrel Hill.

We jus' moved into Bubbie's place from our old 'partment, which was too cold and small for a new baby an' me, Mommy says. I had to sleep on the horsehair couch that scratched me 'cause the sheet wou'nt stay on. An' Mommy had to help me go to the bathroom at night and put on the light, and all the black bugs big as my hand would go runnin' under the toilet.

"We will move to my mother! Before the baby comes." My mother was real loud 'bout movin'.

Daddy got angry and started throwin' dishes on the floor. But when my mommy starts to cry he said, "OK. But just until her third floor people move out. That's it!"

We have to stay with Bubbie 'cause there's other people on the top floor who have somethin' called a leash, I guess like on a dog. Which means I have to sleep with Bubbie squooshed against the wall and listen to her nose soundin' like a horn on the street. She has to pee all the time at night in the middle of sleepin' into a white pot under the bed, and it really smells by morning. But it's lots better than itchin' from the sofa and watchin' the black bugs. I was real 'fraid of those uglies. So we was just almost moved when Mommy had to go to the hostible. Now, after sayin' 'bye to Mommy and my new baby sister, I go to Grandma and Grandpa's house on Phillips Avenue.

Grandma and Grandpa live in a real nice new half double, they call it, after not havin' a place with a inside toilet. Grandma used to take me to the outside toilet at night in the old place, and I had to spread paper on the wood seat and make there and use teared up newspaper to wipe myself. I hated walkin' in the wet grass goin' there in the dark night not bein' able to see anything not even the round hole. You just had to feel for it.

Now, there it is—a real toilet that you jiggle to get the poops down and a tub for taking a bath. I din't understan' why we jus' couldn't stay with Grandma on her third floor. 'Cept Aunt Elaine and Uncle Sam sleep up there all the time. I know Daddy for sure is not happy stayin' with Bubbie and keeps savin' money to get a *place of our own* he says. So here I am gettin' to sleep in Grandpa's room on the day bed with real soft sheets and a big feather quilt and a soft pillow. An' Grandma pulls down blinds that show shadows from the trees and lights from automobiles that go up and down the hill. An' I don't have tuh pee outside at all.

Grandma makes me hot Ovaltine for breakfast and toast out of the oven with lots of butter and jelly. Some days I get a boiled egg just like Grandpa, who cracks it on the side of the bowl and scoops out the runny stuff. I love it 'cause Grandma breaks up the toast in the bowl and I can lick the yellow off my fingers.

"*Nein*, Sorahlah! No licking of your fingers. Use your spoon."

And she takes a wet flour sack towel and wipes my fingers. And then she wipes my face and kisses my nose and says, "Ahi, my *shayna punim*—my *shaynical!*"

Aunt Elaine says that means "my pretty face—my little beauty." I wait every day for Grandma to wipe my face and my hands and plant her kiss. I get egg or jelly on my nose jus' so Grandma can wipe it off. It makes me not so lonesome for Mommy and my new baby sister, who by now is almost a month old. Two weeks have become a month. Mommy can't call me 'cause there's no phone at Bubbie's. Daddy comes only one time a week to eat and take home food to Mommy. Aunt Elaine and Grandma go on a streetcar all the way once tuh see the new baby, but they make me stay home with Grandpa 'cause I have a snotty nose.

I enjoy Grandma's soup and *challah* on Friday. And she lets me go down Phillips Avenue with her to buy fresh bologna and hotdogs at the Hebrew National Deli. Then we go to Ross's market for fruit and vegetables. Grandma takes lots of time looking at them and picks out ones that have fuzzy stuff and gets it cheaper, she says. "We need to watch our *gelt*, Sorahlah." She is real happy when I find a penny lying on the floor, and she spits on it and wipes it on her apron under her coat.

Last we visit Grandpa in the chicken store. Grandma says, "He is the *shoichet* here. That means he is in charge of killing the chickens the right way—the kosher way." Grandma points to one clucking chicken, and she nods at Grandpa. Next thing I know that chicken is living in the basement and I get to spread paper on the floor and give the chicken corn to eat. I like the basement 'cause Grandma has big barrels full of pickles and cabbage getting done. It smells so good!

"Don't touch the big crocks," Grandma warns me. "They are heavy and might fall on you!" I peek inside one and see lots of cabbage and chunks of rye bread. "The bread helps make the cabbage sour for stuffed cabbage, which we will have for dinner when it gets colder," Grandma 'splains. I love to watch Grandma roll the cabbage full of grinded up chicken and some meat. She lets me poke my finger in the end to make the roll stay tight.

Mostly, I am learning how Grandpa *dahvens* every morning and practices for singing at his *shul*, the Poale Zedeck Synagogue. They call him Rabbi there. I hear such a sound and listen and try to make my voice do the same thing. This makes Grandpa very mad.

"Malvina, take her out of here! No singing from girls."

Grandma without saying anything removes me from the dining room where Grandpa is singing. "Sorahlah, go outside and play in the yard." And then I hear her say to Grandpa, "*Apouca*, take her to *shul* with you. She needs to sit with the women and learn to pray and *dahven*, too. It is good for her to learn her place."

And so, on Saturday evening, Grandma gives me a bath; puts on my only dress, which is just fresh worshed and ironed, and my buckle shoes; plaits my hair; and turns me over to my grandpa.

I am so 'cited to walk with my hand in Grandpa's. He is singing real quiet.

"Why don't you sing the words out loud, Grandpa?"

"I am just humming to warm up my voice."

"Is it cold?" I stop and wait for Grandpa to answer me, but he pulls my hand and makes me keep walking.

"Singers need to tune up before they sing." He returns to humming. I start humming, too. "Don't, Sorahlah! You make me lose my place."

I don' know what all that means so I jus' keep hoppin' 'side Grandpa and jumpin' over every crack on the sidewalk. I try kickin' some leaves that are already falling off the trees. But Grandpa jerks me along. An' then there we are. The *shul* is a yellow building with wide doors. Inside it is real dark and feels cold and smells funny.

"Stay still right on this spot. I need to use the toilet—the men's room."

Grandpa disappears into a dimly lit room where I can hear water running, and I recognize the jiggle of a toilet. Then I get the funny smell just like when Bubbie made in the white pot. I see three men come out zipping up their pants. Grandpa comes out and puts on his *tallis*, his *yarmulke* and takes a black book—a *siddur* in his hands. He is still humming.

"Sorahlah, go up the steps with the other women. You can see from the balcony."

I see women are walking up the steps and so I follow. I take a seat down in front where I can lean over the balcony. The women have hats or scarves over their heads and are busy shushing each other—sometimes laughing and covering their mouths with their hands. Then suddenly, I hear it! Grandpa's voice! Singing the words out loud—louder than in the dining room. I am opening my mouth and start to sing with him when he turns and glares at me from the *bima.*

"*Shah!*" A woman next to me sits me down real hard on the wooden bench, and I know I better not make a sound again. She keeps giving me an ugly face. Now I can't see Grandpa at all. So I leave the row and all the women turn and say at once, "*Shah!* Go outside—now."

I run down the steps practically falling over my shoe, and I can see Grandpa through an open door straight down the middle. He is *dahven*ing just like at home— singing and knee bending and weaving back and forth. And all the men are wearing yarmulkes on their heads and are wrapped in *tallises*—"their prayer shawls," Grandma calls them—and doing 'zactly what Grandpa is doing. I do not know why I'm not 'lowed to do it, too.

Then I see an old man carrying a white cloth and bottles come up the stairs behind me. He has a *yarmulke* on his head and a white apron tied 'round his belly. His hands are shaky and wrinkly just like my little sister's hands when she got born. He has huge horn-rimmed glasses over his nose. He spreads the cloth on a long wooden table in the hall, puts the bottles down, and goes into a cupboard under the stairs and brings out glasses, napkins, and brown bags with more stuff. He sets a long *challah* on a plate and throws a napkin over it with a knife to the side, just like Grandma does for *Shabbes* dinner. He empties the brown bag. I see *kichel* with sugar and some with raisins, too, which Grandma always has in her cupboard. There is *mandelbrot*, same as she serves her pinochle ladies, and squares of *matzoh*. Then something new for my nose: jars of onions and slices of something with juice that smells like when Grandma rinses my hair with vinegar. It smells like the pickles in the basement.

I go to the table and dip my finger into the liquid. I suck! *Mmmm...sweet and sour and fishy.* I pick up a piece of the fishy stuff and pop it quick in my mouth before the man grabs my arm and pulls me away from the table.

"'Scuse me, little girl. Stay away from the food. That's all there is, so no tasting! It's for the men!"

"Why for the men?"

"Huh? If you need to pish, go down to the ladies toilet at the bottom of the steps."

"Why's the food jus' for the men?"

"We have a big *minyon* tonight and are short on pickled herring."

He goes back into the cupboard, and I use the opportunity to break off a piece of *challah* and go for the herring plate. I put a piece of the fish in my mouth with the bread full of juice quick 'fore he comes back. My mouth and nose like the onions and juice. I swallow just in time.

"I told you to stay away from the food! Why are you here? Who do you belong to?"

I point to Grandpa. "My grandpa is the singer...the rabbi."

"So? Go sit with the women upstairs where you belong." Then he hears Grandpa singing the *Adonolom*. "Never mind, the service is almost done. Wait over there for the women. And stay out of the herring. Your hands will *ge shtink*!" Then he goes into the bathroom and I can hear the jiggle and smell that white pot smell. I lick my hands clean as I can.

The bright colored *shul* windows are all black now. Grandpa's on the *bima* and lights the twisted blue and white *Havdalah* candle just like he does at home. I know the smell of the wax dripping on the plate. *Shabbes* is over for sure. At home, Grandma will set the table for a Saturday night dinner of *cholent* and fresh *challah* and all kinds of cakes with hot tea. Grandma 'lows me to drink the tea and dip *kichel* into the honeypot on the table. "For a sweet week," she says.

The old men are running to the bathroom. The jiggling is loud and the smell is terrible. The men go right over to the table, open the bottles and pour out what they say is wine, and lift glasses up and shout, "*L'chayim, l'chayim!*" Then they dig into the food. They shake Grandpa's hand, wishing him "*Gut Shabbes und a gutn vokh.*" They tell him how wonderful he does the service. My mouth wants to taste the herring again! I try to squeeze past the men, but they push me out.

I go and stand by the open door with the women looking out into the night. They say, "Good *Shabbes, gut Shabbes und a gutn vokh*—a good week," to each other and walk real quick down the steps and up the street. I guess they gotta get home so they kin get their *cholent* and *challah* ready for dinner. I wait by the door for Grandpa. He takes my sticky hand in his and we cross the street. His hand *ge shtinks* from herring!

Chapter Two

THE LIBRARY CARD
AUGUST 1938

I'm about five an' a half an' my nose doesn't look like the other noses in the rest of the fam'ly. My mother says it's a little button.

"Don't worry," Grandma says. "It will grow into your face."

I don't understand what she means. She covers it with smushy kisses calling me her "*shayna punim*"—pretty face.

Grandpa and Uncle Sam have huge beaks like the eagle on the 'merican flag at the post office. Daddy has a broken nose that's always red and swollen. Grandma says he got it broke in a fight hitchin' on a vegetable truck in California when he ran away from home. Daddy says, "It got broke when I fell off the back of the truck. I was tryin' to make my fortune. What an adventure!" Then Uncle Sam starts yelling, "Your '*adventure*', dear brother, cost the family a fortune!" This starts a fight between my uncle and father with arms flying over my head. I cover my eyes. Grandma steps into the middle of the two. Grandpa grabs me outta the way, pulling me tight to his chest. I'm scared my nose will be broken like Daddy's when Grandpa hugs me. His arms bury me 'gainst his vest buttons leaving little round rings on my face, my nose turns red, and my hair crackles and stands out. *Am I gonna get indented or 'lectrocuted?*

Later on, after everybody is back to regular, Uncle Sam tries to twist and pinch my nose or any other part of me he can find. "That nose doesn't belong in this family," he declares. "Let's pull it out!" He does his best to make me cry. Crying in front of my father or uncle only makes them torture me more. I put my hands over my face so Uncle Sam can't grab my nose. Then he tries for my ears.

Grandma tells me, "Forget it. They'll stop it soon."

Mommy tells me my nose is just perfect. "Anyway," she says, "noses are for smelling roses and for letting you know if dinner's a winner." That makes me laugh. Mommy can rhyme for anything. "A good sniffer, big or small, is an advantage over all. Besides, being nosy runs in the family on both sides." That makes Grandma real mad.

It's August! Thirty days before kindergarten starts. Mommy shows me how to put a big *X* on the calendar for each day. I can't wait. Going to school and reading real books is my dream. Mommy practices rhyming with me every day.

"Okay, Sorahlah, the word is *cat* and it rhymes with…"

"Rat," I jump in, "and with mat, hat, and bat."

"Oh, you're going to be good in school, my Sorahlah!"

Mommy calls me Sorahlah, my Jewish name, when she's proud of me and follows it with a kiss on my nose. She uses Shirley, my got borned name, to make me listen when I'm too busy playing with my paper dolls.

"Shirley, do you hear me? I've called you ten times already. It's dinnertime. Shirley Ruth!" When she adds my middle name I know I better answer.

Now suddenly my nose answers for me! I smell the chicken soup or fried potatoes or the roasted meat. I bounce into the kitchen. "Mmmm! Mommy, can I have soup with lots of noodles, please—and carrots, too?"

"Sit! Your father is late! You can have soup and all the noodles you want. The meat's for tomorrow's dinner after we get home from the library."

She takes a large ladle and stirs the soup, plops a spoonful of noodles in a deep bowl, and pours the soup carefully over them, adding carrots. "Blow! The soup's hot," she says.

I begin to stir, blow, and taste the soup with the tip of my tongue on the spoon. "Liberry? You didn't tell me we're going to the liberry. What for?"

"There's a summer story hour this month. I want someone besides me reading to you. It will help you get ready for school.

And the word is *library*, Sorahlah." She names the letters and pronounces it slowly.

I'm real happy when Mommy reads stories and writes down rhyming words I make up. "These are your poems, Shirley." She puts them in a lined book with a blue cover.

"Will you read the story at the liberry?"

"They have a woman—a librarian—in charge. She will read aloud and ask questions. You'll feel what it's like to be with other children who are listening, too."

"Will she write down my pomes?"

"It's not like that. You'll learn how to pay attention and take books home."

"Can I read by myself?"

"Well, that will take a little more time!" And she grabs me, planting a very hard kiss on one cheek and finally right on my nose, almost spilling the hot soup on my lap.

The next day I'm up way before Mommy with my best shoes and dress and my hair ready to be plaited.

"Sorahlah! That is your good dress and shoes. You need to change." Then she sees my face and stops. "OK. Just don't sit on the floor or scuff your shoes. Bring me the brush and gum bands so I can plait your hair."

I sit while she brushes, only grunting once when she pulls out the knots and tightens the gum bands at the end.

"Too tight," I complain.

"They will loosen in the heat! Let's go. It will take a good hour to walk to the library."

It's a warm day. My new shoes feel stiff as I hopscotch over the cracks.

"Step on a crack—break your mother's back! That rhymes doesn't it, Mommy?"

"Absolutely, Sorahlah! But be careful with your new shoes!"

We walk past the Belmar Movie House and Greengard's Hardware Store, and across Homewood Avenue. "This is the *H* street." Mommy points to the sign above us.

As we come to a busy street, Mommy holds my hand tightly.

"I can cross by myself," I insist.

"Just hold my hand, young lady. You're not grown yet."

"Young lady" is even stronger than Shirley to get my attention. It works.

The blue sky has white clouds shaped like faces with very big noses. I look up, trying to jump the sidewalk cracks at the same time, and suddenly—plunk. I go down next to Mommy's legs.

"Shirley Ruth! Look what you've done, young lady."

Uh, oh! My middle name, too!

One patent leather shoe has a scratch and my dress hem is ripped. Worse, there's a red scrape on my knee. But, I don't cry. I do not cry. Whimper. But I don't give into tears even though it hurts something awful. Mommy fusses, picks me up, and spits on her hanky to clean off the scrape. "Ouch!" I squeak.

"Oh, well! I shouldn't have let you wear new shoes on a long walk. You'll survive. Come on, we'll be late for story hour." She grabs my hand pulling me to keep up with her. We cross another street, pass a grocery and boys pulling red wagons filled with newspapers. I try to turn to see them.

"Eyes ahead, Sor. Walk faster."

The sun is heating up my head. My face's all wet. I run to keep up with Mommy, but I jump the cracks anyway. I lick my lips. *Yucky—salt.* Suddenly we stop at steps going up to two large glass doors with gold shining metal. The building is red brick with high windows. Other children and parents are in front of us.

"Are we there yet?" I practically yell.

"Uh huh, but speak softly inside." Mommy jerks me through the door. It bangs shut.

"Huh? Why?" I've never been to the liberry before. The large space swallows me up. The ceiling goes real high with big curves in the wall just like the Holy Rosary Church next to our house. Twisted ropes hold lights with yellow glass. They tremble when the front door bangs.

"Quiet, please!" says a woman behind a high wooden desk.

She is busy opening and closing books, pulling out little white cards, and making a thud noise with a red-handled piece of wood.

She says, "Shhh!" again with a very mad look on her face and puts her finger to her lips. A young boy pushes a tall wooden wagon with books piled up over to her, and motions. She nods and takes the books, looks inside each one, pulls a card out and thud, pulls a card and thud. Out, thud; out, thud. My mommy is busy talking to a man dressed like a policeman.

"Oh," she says. "Thank you."

I begin to feel the quiet and the way everyone walks—hardly moving, almost floating. But most special is the smell! Every time the lady at the desk opens a book, the smell fills my nose. That smell's everywhere.

"Take my hand, Sorahlah. The reading room's this way."

"Why do I have to hold your hand? We're not crossing the street."

"Shirley!"

It's not a voice to argue with. We head down a hallway with hard stone floors following other children into a room.

"Look, Mommy, my size chairs an' a table an' books!" I point at a large poster. "What does the sign say?"

She whispers, "*Story hour today—eleven a.m. for children entering kindergarten and first grade.* Go sit down with the other children, Sorahlah." My mother relaxes her grip. "I'll come back for you when the clock says twelve." She points to the clock over the door. My tummy is jumbling. Mommy never leaves me without somebody I know. I start to follow her.

"No, Shirley, you need to stay without me. You're a big girl getting ready to go to school by yourself. I'll be right in the next room where they have grownup books. You'll be fine. And pay attention to the librarian." She points at another woman who is holding a large yellow book in her hands and standing near the children.

I can feel my heart beating; my eyes follow Mommy as she disappears down the hall.

"Please, children, sit down and let's get ready for story hour. I see some new faces here today." The woman—the liberrian—looks straight at me. "Tell me your name, child."

Does she mean me? No one has ever called me "child" before. Then I see everybody looking right at me. "Uh, name? Sorah—uh, I mean Shirley. I'm Shirley." I don't recognize my own voice. It sounds distant and soft and not at all like me.

"You have to speak up, Shirley, so everyone can hear you. The library is a large room; we need to speak up."

That seems silly since the other lady in the hallway keeps shushing everyone.

"Shirley," I say in what mommy calls my outside voice.

"Not quite that much!" The liberrian smiles. "Is this your first trip to the library?"

"Uh huh." I nod and pull at my dress. Then I bravely add, "I like the way the liberry smells." The other children start to laugh, but the liberrian quickly puts her finger to her lips and they immediately stop. My face feels funny and hot. I plop into the nearest chair.

"I'm Miss Schaeffer, Shirley. Welcome to our story hour."

She pulls up a small chair and joins us. She puts her knees together carefully, folding her flowered dress over her legs. She rests the book on her lap. I can see there's a picture of a man with white hair holding a funny looking doll on the front of the book cover. The doll has a button nose like mine. There are strings attached to his arms and head.

Miss Schaeffer begins. "This is the story of Pinocchio, a wooden doll who wants to become a real boy! I'm going to show you the pictures first and tell you part of the story. Then I'll start to read to you. You must learn to listen. What do you see on the cover?"

A girl blurts out the answer. "I know, teacher, iss a puppet…"

The liberrian stops her. "Mary, you need to raise your hand if you want to speak." Mary raises her hand and goes right on.

"I know this story already. Tha's his father. He loves Pinocchio and wants him to be—uh, uh—"

"Mary, do you remember the father's name?" Miss Schaeffer waits for the answer.

"I don' know." Mary shrugs and looks down at the floor.

"Gepetto. The father of Pinocchio is Gepetto. Watch how I write his name on the blackboard." Then she takes a piece of chalk and writes on a large board near her chair, saying each letter, "G-E-P-E-T-T-O."

I look at the letters but can't figure out why she does that. She begins showing pictures from the book and asking us about the pictures. She reads, stops, and asks a question. I wish she would just tell the story. Then suddenly, I'm stuck with my mouth open as she turns the page. There's Pinocchio with a nose shaped like a carrot.

"Oh, my!" I yell.

"What's wrong, Shirley? Do you have something to say?" The liberry lady looks right at me. "Raise your hand."

I raise my hand to my own nose. "His nose, his nose! What happened to his little button nose?"

"Well, that is part of the story," she says. "When he tells a lie his nose starts…"

My hand goes up. "Is that how your nose grows into your face?" I ask.

The liberrian looks puzzled. Then she shows the next picture. Pinocchio's nose is back to its own button size. I let out a big breath! The liberrian continues. "Now, boys and girls, listen to the whole story and see if you know why Pinocchio's nose changes and what happens to him."

I'm glad we are finally going to hear the story without questions. The liberrian uses her own voice and then tries to sound like Gepetto or Pinocchio or the carnival man. Everyone laughs. *Why's that so funny? I play the pretending game with Mommy lots of times. We always use funny voices.*

The story is long. My dress is stuck to me. I rub the scrape on my knee, spitting on my finger. Other parents are sitting with children away from me, looking through books. My mouth is thirsty. I feel my eyes closing. *Is it twelve yet?* Suddenly the liberrian calls my name.

"Shirley—Shirley! What do you think of that? Why does his nose grow longer?" She waits patiently for me to answer. "Shirley?" I feel like I just got woke up.

"Ooh, ooh, I know, I know." A boy wildly waves his hand.

"Yes, David."

"Ef'ry time he lies his nose grows and then he's a real boy and din't have a long nose anymore and stays home to play with his toys and…"

"Thank you, David. Now, Shirley, do you understand?"

I nod and quickly feel my nose. I am lying. Will my nose change, too?

The liberry lady continues. "Now those of you who already have your library card may go to the shelves and find a book you would like to take home and read. Remember! The book you take is due back in one week. That's seven days from now. Make sure you can count off the days on your calendars at home!"

I smile 'cause I already know how to do that. Then I see my mommy. I wave frantically, jumping up and running across the stone floor. Oops! Down I go! My other shoe gets a scuff. The whole hem of my dress hangs down.

"No running allowed in the library," the liberrian whispers. "Are you hurt, Shirley?"

My mommy helps me up and answers for me. "I'm sure she's fine. Just a little excited to take a book home."

"Well, that's a wonderful kind of excitement. I'm Miss Schaeffer. You will need to fill out a permission form to take out books, and Shirley must sign her name to a special library card." The liberrian opens a drawer in the desk and takes out a paper and pencil. "Shirley. Let me see you sign your name."

I rub my shoe up and down my other leg. Mommy smiles her best mother smile and speaks in a soft voice. "Can I take the books out on my card, Miss Schaeffer? Shirley hasn't learned to sign her name yet. And…"

The liberrian interrupts. "That is not the purpose of the card. Children must learn to value their word through their signature. Shirley should be able to sign her name. Even if you read the book to her, she must be responsible for the care and return of the book. Just fill in the basic information, address, phone number on this special sheet and…" The liberry lady hands Mommy a card telling her what to do.

"Oh." Mommy takes the card in her hand and fills in the sheet. "I will see that she learns to write her name, and then we'll return and take out books. OK, Shirley?"

I nod. I already practice my name at the back of my blue book of poems. I'll have my name perfect by the next story time. Mommy fills in the information on the sheet and takes the card for me to sign. "Good-bye, and thank you," Mommy says.

The liberrian nods. She is taking cards out of books and thudding each card before she hands the book back to a waiting child. "Remember! Seven days on the calendar."

"What's she doin', Mommy? What's those cards for?"

Mommy pulls me out and back down the hallway. I twist around watching the liberry lady thud, thud, thud.

"Those are check-out cards. You write your name on the card and the librarian stamps the date they are due back on the card inside the pocket of the book. She uses an inkpad and a stamp with the date on it. When they are returned, she stamps them again."

"An ink pad?" I screw up my nose. "Boy, it smells!"

"You smell black ink and books; books have a special smell, especially when they are used and old."

"The chalk smells, too," I add, feeling very smart. "My hopscotch chalk smells just like that."

Mommy laughs. "When you go to school there will be lots of smells—books, chalk." And she adds, "And lots of teacher talk!"

"Will I get stinky ink?" That makes Mommy laugh even more. "It rhymes, huh, Mommy?"

"Almost a perfect rhyme! After you learn to read, you'll have a pen and an inkwell and paper to practice on."

I skip happily past the large desk where the other lady is thud-thudding. Mommy grabs my hand as we open the big doors; the smell of the library fades. Outside the sun is a yellow circle in the sky, blinding my eyes. I bury my face under Mommy's arm. I'm thinking about signing the library card. "Mommy, can you buy me a new pencil and paper so's I can practice my name?"

Suddenly she stops walking. "You know, Sorahlah, right now things are tight. Your father's sales are not good and..." Then she looks down at me and smiles. "When we get to Greengard's Hardware Store, I'll buy you a lined writing tablet and some pencils just like they use in school. You'll be able to practice all you want." Mommy begins singing a song while she carefully steps over the cracks in the sidewalk.

"Step on a crack, break you mother's back! Step in a hole, ruin your leather soles. So now you make one up, too," she laughs.

And that's what we do. Taking turns, laughing and rhyming—walking frontward and backwards until we get to Greengard's. My mommy goes to the office where Mr. Greengard sits. I look over the notebooks and settle on a black cover and some yellow pencils. Then I spy a small square chalkboard with a box of chalk. I put my nose to the board and then to the chalk. It smells like the liberry. Mommy lets me have all the things and signs a little yellow pad, which Mr. Greengard stamps just like the liberry lady with a thud. He puts the items in a bag and hands them to me.

"I'm really pleased to help a nice young lady learn to write her name, Shirley."

"I'm gonna practice right away," I announce.

Mommy nods and seems quite pleased with herself.

"Let's hurry home, Sorahlah, before Bubbie gets tired of sitting with your sister." We need to get there before Daddy, too."

Daddy's pleased about roast with gravy and mashed potatoes for dinner. But he isn't happy 'bout my notebook and stuff.

"You know, Lil, we don't have money for extras. You have no business charging. It'll have to be paid for by September with interest."

I go into my bedroom and shut the door to drown out the yelling. I spread my new pencils on the floor sharpening them with the little red blade Mr. Greengard had thrown in for free. Everyday I write a line of S-S-S-H-H-H I-I-I-R-R-R L-L-L-E-E-E-Y-Y-Y. I try it out on the chalkboard, too. When "*Shirley*" is perfect, I begin on my last name. I show Mommy how each letter stands straight and tall on the little broken blue lines—evenly spaced with a finger between them just like she showed me.

"Wonderful, Shirley. But we will have to wait another week for the library. I need to help your father with his orders this week."

"But, Mommy, the story hour!"

"I'm sorry, Sorahlah. Your father's business comes first." She pats me on the head, which is not usual for my mother. No kiss? But then, I have a real good idea. *I can write my name, I know about the liberry, and—well, why not? No need to bother Mommy. She has a lot to do with Daddy and cooking and cleaning and getting me ready for school 'n taking care of Barbara Lea. I'll show her ah'm a big girl.*

The next morning, I put on my slightly scuffed patent shoes and the dress Mommy has fixed, and take the liberry card from her purse. I sit down at the table and carefully put my name on an empty line. Then I slip out the front door, trying not to let the door bang, and take off down the street. I start hopping over the cracks. I sing the rhymes Mommy and me made up. I pass the Belmar Movie feeling very good about being in charge of myself. I see the hardware store. Mr. Greengard's outside sweeping the sidewalk. I wave at him, and he scratches his head as he waves back.

"Where's your mother?" he shouts. But I keep right on going until I get to the corner.

Is this Homewood Avenue? I look up at the sign hanging on a pole. The street name begins with an *H. But where's the grocery store? What happened to the grocery store? Oh, my!* Then suddenly the cars will not stop whizzing by. Every time I decide to cross, a horn honks.

Then I feel a hand on my shoulder. "Do you need help crossing?" A man does not wait for me to answer but takes my hand and then just picks me up and carries me 'cross the street. When he sets me down he points up at the lights on each corner. "You need to watch for green to cross and red to stop. Where's your mother, little girl? Why are you out on Hamilton by yourself?"

"Hamilton? Where's Homewood? I thought this was the *H* letter street."

He speaks to me very quietly. "They both start with an H. Home-wood and Hamilton. Homewood is around the corner. You must have missed the turn. Where are you supposed to be?"

"I'm gonna' meet my mother at the liberry," I say in my outside voice and show him my liberry card. Then I touch my nose.

"You better get on the other side of this street and turn the next corner and stay straight on. Don't get lost." He picks me up, carries me again to the other corner, puts me down, points me in the right direction, and says, "Just follow your nose! And don't talk to strangers like me!"

I start walking faster. I don't wanna be late. *Jus' follow my nose? How can you follow your nose?* I stay close to the buildings away from the traffic and make the turn. It seems forever. My feet hurt. *What if this isn't the right way? What if ah'm lost! What if I can't find the big doors with shiny metal? What if?* Then there it is—the liberry. My heart's pounding. My face is sweaty. My mouth feels like Daddy washed it with soap for saying a bad word. Other children are going inside the door, but it shuts before I can squeeze in. The door's too heavy for me to grab at the bottom.

Finally, a tall boy opens it and I hurry past him. The quiet, the soft light, the coolness inside feel good. The same lady is stamping the cards, stacking the books, and stamping—thud, thud, thud. I hold my liberry card tight in my hand and find the story room.

The chairs are in a circle. On each chair the liberry lady is putting a pink paper with a picture of the little wooden boy, Pinocchio, sitting and reading a book. I walk over to a bookshelf and look at the books. I can name the letters on the cover but not the words. One thing is for sure: I can smell those books. I put my nose close up to the pages of a thick book off the bottom shelf. It's real heavy, and with my library card in one hand, I drop it—splat. There it is with words looking up at me. If only I could read those words.

"Children, take a seat." Miss Schaeffer is writing in big letters on the chalkboard and notices me right away. She comes over and puts the book back on the shelf. "Shirley, how nice to see you again. Ah, you have your library card." She takes it right out of my hand and examines it closely. "Is this your printing? What a good job. You certainly are ready to take out books." I keep nodding yes; she keeps staring at the card. "But where's your mother's signature? You signed on the wrong line. Oh, never mind. When your mother picks you up, we'll fill out a new card."

A new card! When my mother picks me up! How do I handle this big lie? I feel my nose. It's still a button. I sit down on a chair really hard. If the liberry lady reads a story, I don't hear a word. I fiddle with my dress. I scrape my shoe across the floor and wrap a leg around the chair bottom. I suck on the end of my plait, which is undone without a gum band. My hands are black with pencil from my name on the card. I feel my heart and tummy squishin'.

Suddenly, the story is over. I'm happy that today the questions are for other children. Miss Schaeffer adds, "Take home the pink sheet. It lists some books for your parents to read to you."

Then I stand up and run for the door.

"Shirley! Shirley," the liberrian calls. It's an outside voice—definitely. "Just a minute, please, young lady." That stops me! "Where's your mother?"

"Uh, I guess she forgot to come for me, uh, or, uh…!"

She grabs my hand tightly and takes me to the desk and sits me on a chair, which twirls around. My tummy is getting sick.

"Stay right here and don't move. Do you hear me?" She does not wait for my answer but marches to the back of the reading room. I see her on the telephone.

Suddenly there are one, two, then a whole bunch of tears running down my face. My nose is leaking out, too. I try to wipe my nose with the hem of my dress; my decision not to let anybody see me cry is not working. The liberrian takes my hand and leads me into a room with grown-up tables, a sink, and a small icebox. She takes a flowered hanky out of her sleeve and wets it with cool water. She wipes my face and looks into my eyes.

"Blow," she says. And I do right into her wet hanky.

"You're a very determined little girl, Shirley. Your parents are coming for you. Luckily, I had your mother's information sheet from last week. She had no idea where you were! They were about to call the police."

She goes to the icebox and takes out a small bottle of milk, pours it in a glass, and opens a package of crackers that sit on her desk.

"Here, you must be ravenous."

I don't know what that means. My stomach makes noises and my head hurts. I gobble the crackers and drink the milk so fast it dribbles down my chin onto my good dress.

"Why didn't you wait for your mother?"

I wipe my chin off with my hand and tell her how I practiced and was gonna show my mother I was a big girl. When I get to the part about the man carrying me 'crost the street, she moans and turns a funny color.

"Oh, Shirley, you should not let a stranger pick you up."

"That's what the man said. But I didn't want to miss story hour an' I wanted to show I could write my name on the liberry card. I knew the way, but I got lost on the *H* corner. Can I take a book out now, please?"

"Shirley, you will never get lost! I'm so proud of you. But promise never to walk here without your mother or father again, please. And don't let strangers touch you."

I guess she doesn't think she is a stranger since she gives me a big smushy hug just like my grandpa, and I kin smell the books, ink pad, and Grandma's lilac bush all over her.

"You certainly are ready to take out books this week. Come, we'll pick one together while we wait for your parents." She takes my hand and we go back into the liberry room. She pulls a chair to the bookshelves and shows me books she thinks I'd enjoy. She opens a big book with fancy looking letters and pictures and words, and points to the word under a picture.

"Say the letters out loud, Shirley."

I name each letter. "P-U-M-P-K-I-N?"

"Do you know what's in the picture, Shirley?"

"Thas' a punkin," I answer.

"Yes, Shirley, now you sound out the letters. The letters together say the name of the picture; the picture is a pumpkin. It is the word. Understand?"

I nod and then feel my nose, pretending to scratch it. It's in place.

We look at other P words…puppy…pretzel…then suddenly the pages flip open to a picture of a large piece of bread with lettuce and tomatoes and cheese and pickles and another slice ready to go on top. I gasp and turn the page to see the whole bread going into a large open mouth. On the next page there are the letters.

"S-A-N-D-W-I-C-H!" I say the letters all by myself an' almost fall off the chair.

"That says sam'ich—! Mommy showed me that word at the grocery store. It says sam'ich. Oh, my! I can read. I can read. Sam'ich, sam'ich!"

The liberrian shouts, "That's right! It says sandwich."

"Shh!" a voice whispers loudly.

"Oops!" Miss Schaeffer covers her mouth. "It's hard to be quiet when you're learning to read." She hugs me again.

I know I'm gonna get it good from my father when we get home. I don't care. My nose is full of liberry smells—books, ink, chalk! "My tummy has butterflies jus' like Mommy told me," I explain excitedly to the liberrian. "That's a real special feeling when something new and wonderful happens like now! I can write my name. An' I can read the word *sam'ich* in a book or on a eading menu at Isaly's! Wow! Reading—eading—reading—eading!"

Miss Schaeffer smiles.

"I'm gonna put that rhyme in my pome book first thing."

Chapter Three

THE LITTLE RED WAGON
SEPTEMBER 1939 TO AUGUST 1941

One day I discover you can make music come out of a big clackity box! There it is: a big wooden box they call a pyeano—at Uncle Abe's moving place—way bigger than me! A black mover guy sits down and makes this fast music come out of it. The keys go clackity and his hands move so fast I can hardly see them. But the pyeano has a funny, not-right sound. When the man stands up, he bangs the cover down. I want to make the clackity sound, too, but the auction man starts and I have to sit and be quiet.

Then I go with Mommy to a meeting. There it is: another big box pyeano with the cover up. I know just what to do. I peck with one hand and then with both.

"Sorahlah, what's that music? Are you getting into trouble? I told you not to touch anything. Sorahlah?" Mommy appears at the door. By then my hands are going real fast. "Who showed you how to do that?"

"The radio. Some sisters sing it all the time. I'll be with you in apple blossom time—I'll be with you to dah, dah, dah dah…" *This pyeano goes clackity just like at the auction.*

"How do you do that without any music?"

"I don't know. It's sorta in my head and comes outta my fingers."

Cousin Zelda appears. "My, Sorahlah, really. I can hardly believe it."

A lady with a funny looking hat joins in. "That's talent all right. Didn't know she took lessons."

"Taught herself. She's a very talented child, my Sorahlah." Mommy's smiling with a scrunchy face.

"Give her lessons." Zelda brushes cookie crumbs off her chest.

"We've just moved onto my mother's third floor. There's no money for lessons." Mother closes the lid with a bang.

"We're all struggling right now!" Zelda pins her hat on her head. The meeting is over.

Three weeks later, right after school, I hide behind the curtain in the auditorium. The stage has a big long black pyeano that other children get to put their fingers on. It isn't clackity at all.

"Good-bye, children! Don't forget to practice every day." I know this lady shows children how to play the pyeano every Tuesday. She closes her notebook and sticks her pencil right into a funny knot on top of her head just like my bubbie does at the candy store.

"Oh!" She catches me. "Who are you? Don't hide. Come out here, please!"

"I just wanted tuh watch. How do yah get a turn on the, uh—pyeano?"

"You mean the lessons?" She gathers her books and then stops. "What grade are you in?"

"Grade one."

She opens the brown notebook again. "What is your name, please?" She takes the pencil out of her hair and taps the page.

"Sorahlah. Uh…" I try to look at her writing.

"Can you read?"

I hang my head and shrug my shoulders.

"No, no. Can you read in your regular class?"

"I can read *Dick and Jane* by mem'ry. An' I kin play 'Apple Blossom Time.'"

"Really? Show me."

I do what my father calls my parlor trick.

"Who taught you that, *Sarah*—uh—did you say?"

"Shirley…my name's Shirley." I scrape my red buckle shoe up and down my leg. "The music is in my head and it comes outta my fingers." I play the apple song again fast as the pyeano guy.

"My, Shirley." She looks at me kinda funny and then writes my name in her book. "You can begin coming to lessons every Tuesday last period. But you need to bring a quarter for each lesson and seventy-five cents for the book." She holds up a bright red book with a hand on the cover. "Can you remember to tell your parents Miss Allison would like to teach you? You know, you will have to practice."

I know what that means 'cause Mommy makes me practice reading and printing my name on the blue dotted lines. "Yes ma'am. But I don't have no pyeano."

"You can use this until your parents get a piano." She pronounces the word *pihahno* very clearly. "Please don't lose it. It's my last one." She hands me a cardboard that has black and white stripes just like the real clackity.

"But where's the sound?"

"You can pretend to hear and sing and make your fingers go up and down the board." She smoothes out her flowered dress, sits down, and places her hand on the board. "Watch how I do it." She shows me while she sings, *"Here we go…up a row…to a birthday party."* I just do it like her right away but on the real keys. This clackity doesn't sound funny at all.

"Very nice, Shirley. Practice that on the board keys, and I will see you next Tuesday. And please! The instrument is a pihahno, not a pyeano. You will have to learn to speak correctly. My students must be able to announce their pieces at the recital."

Whatever that is, I'll do it. I fly home holding the cardboard keys tightly under my arm. Telling my parents about the money is a big problem. Getting the money every week is an even bigger one. "Mommy, I need a quarter for my lesson tomorrow, please."

"Oh, yes…yes…uh…I have to ask your father. This has been a very bad week."

"But I can't miss another lesson and I owe from last week. I won't be ready for the recital."

"Shhhh! Your father is coming up the steps. *Shah!*"

"What's she whining about now?" Daddy tosses his hat on the kitchen table and takes off his jacket. "Damn hot out there today. Couldn't take in a plugged nickel in this heat." His voice is mad; his face, dripping water. He takes the dishtowel off Mommy's shoulder and wipes his face.

"I need a quarter, Daddy, for my lesson, an' I owe from last week."

"Lil, I told you no lessons. You had no business letting her start in the first place, and that book's useless." He reaches for the book, but I hide it under my dress. "We need the money for important things. I can't even afford a new pair of shoes. Did you polish my black ones, Lil?"

My mother shakes her head as she stirs the pot on the stove. Daddy hangs his tie on the doorknob. "I need to make a good impression on my customers. What do you do around here all day? I'm out there breaking my back…"

"But Mommy promised…"

"I make the rules around here."

"My twenty-five cents, Daddy. She promised."

"The only thing I promise you is a good whippin'."

I run and hide in my bedroom and cover my ears. All I can think of is how to get two quarters. My little sister starts crying in the next room.

September 1940

From then on, I walk to school eyes stuck to the sidewalk look-ing for lost pennies or nickels. People come out of my bubbie's candy store drinking Coke and sometimes leave the bottle on the curb. I know Bubbie grabs those bottles and gets money back at the grocery. Lucky me! I spot two pennies off the curb and two Coke bottles. It's hard holding everything. One of the bottles breaks! I disappear real quick.

The next week, Mommy asks Aunt Mayme for the little red wagon my cousin Sammy doesn't want. It could hold lots of stuff. I grab a bottle before Bubbie can see me and pull my new wagon across the street to the movie theater next to the funeral home. People sometimes leave a bottle on a window ledge. I come up with enough for—I make each finger bend—six cents. "Don't count on your fingers," Mommy says. "Use your head!" Learning to count is awful hard. Speaking right to please my pihahno teacher is harder. But I need those quarters, that's for sure. *"Try Holy Rosary Church again,*" I say to myself. Once before the sisters had a leftover bottle—a big one worth a nickel. I pull the wagon back across the street and park it on the sidewalk and timidly knock on the church door. It swings open a little. I knock harder. I can just see inside the church.

"Sister, get that, please, I'm trying to practice the hymn for Sunday." I know Sister Angelique's voice. I see her feet going up and down at a funny lookin' pihahno, and strange loud music echoes and jumbles my ears.

I knock with both my hands as hard as I can.

"Sister, the door...please!"

"All right, all right. But who would knock at a church door when you can just come in. Coming, I'm coming." Sister Mary Michael's face appears at the door. "Yes, may I help you? Oh, Shirley, it's you. What can I do for you today? I gave you all the empties we had last week. We don't have anymore." She turns to walk away.

"But, Sister, you told me that if I pray the right way—inside the church, to—to—um?"

"To Jesus, child, to Jesus. That's whom you need to pray to. You will soon see the true light, little one. Put your hand in the holy water. It is blessed. Then I promise you, Jesus will hear your prayer."

Sister grabs my hand and pulls me towards a white marble bird bath.

I splash as the sister pushes my hand into the water. "Ugh—it's cold." My voice is weak. I sputter as I get it all over myself. It makes me shiver.

"Tell me what is it you seek, my child. Tell the good Lord. Don't be afraid. You have to recognize Jesus, the Son of God, openly." The music gets louder; Sister Angelique's hands and feet are going faster. Sister Mary Michael tries to push me to my knees.

"Oh! It's dark in here." I cover my ears and struggle away from her and start to back out.

"Don't be timid child! Jesus will love you even if you are Jewish." She grabs my arm. I squirm. She holds me tight. "Tell me what is it you seek, my child. Tell the good Lord. Pray!"

"A quarter for my lesson. I—I—" Then suddenly I feel a coin pressed into my hand. "Oh, Sister, thank you, thank you."

"Thank Jesus, child. He answered your prayer. Praise Jesus! Praise the Lord."

Sister Angelique begins singing even louder. The music makes my feet tickle. I run out, brushing the smelly water off my dress. The sudden bright sunlight makes me blink. I grab the handle of my wagon. It jangles across the street, almost dumping my bottle. My hand presses against my dress pocket. The quarter is safe.

The Saturday movie crowd is letting out. I spot two more Coke bottles on the ledge of the stones under the giant picture of *King Kong*. Four more cents! I count on my fingers to figure out how many empties it will take to make another quarter. Suddenly, I see a glint of light under the wheel of a parked car. A dime! It's a dime with a funny looking lady waving at me. *Thank you, thank you, whoever dropped that dime.* I look lovingly at my red wagon and its bottles. *Thank you, thank you.* I want to say, "Praise Lord Jesus," but then I bite my tongue.

November 1941

One morning, about two months into the lessons and way behind in my quarters, I'm watching the storefront for my bubbie, who pays me a penny to help her. I notice a large cardboard sign with funny holes in it. I take the sign and try to figure which way to read it. A pointy stick hangs by a string from the sign.

"*Vas toost du?*" Bubbie is tying a big white apron over her long blue dress. A yellow pencil is stuck in her hair knot. She grabs the sign from me and puts it back on the counter.

"I'm trying to see what it says. *Be the l-l—uc-ky, lucky win-ner... take a chance...raaaff-fles twenty-five cents.* Twenty-five cents? Raffles?"

"*Du reedst* already! Better you should learn to count."

"What's a raffle?"

"A *mishugenah* game. *Du macht a loch*—a hole—*mit dis.*" She holds the pointy stick by its string. "*Ich weis nicht* in English. *Unt den du ken* maybe get a dollar. *De ganze vinner hat ein vatch.* I don' believe it, doh! Dere is no vinner ever. Only *deine tatah ist de vinner.*"

He takes de money ven de punch board ist done. He vill always be a *schlepper*! No goot ever. Better he should *gib tsu mir dah* rent he owess. *Min tochter hat a peckele.*" She makes funny noises with her false teeth and blows her nose in a rolled-up handkerchief. *I just keep nodding the whole time Bubbie's talkin' just like Mommy tells me to do.* "We all have a hard time with her mish mash of English and German and Yiddish, "my mommy adds.

"How d'ya know you vin, uh I mean win?" *I'm sounding like Bubbie!*

"It on de paper inside de *loch*—de hole. *Ich kennst redn tsu dir.* I need tuh go in de back.Vatch de front! *Und chap nit*—don' take any ting fom de candy!" I nod again and help myself to some licorice as soon as Bubbie's out of sight.

Why does Daddy have to wait for the money? I will do it for him. I take the pointy stick and punch out a hole. I read the words really quick. *Sorry, better luck next time. Try again.* I try again. *Better luck next time.* Next time? Again? *You have just won two chances for the price of one.* What does that mean? Oh, well. Better luck next—where's the dollar? Where's the vatch? I don't understand. This game is no fun.

Bubbie has a fit, what my mother calls a conniption fit, when she sees the little papers on the floor. "*Vat hast du gethun? Deine tatah vilst macht du* a vippin fer sure! Oy, yoy, yoy! Dis vill cost a *ganze veek's gelt.* Sorahlah!" I don't have any trouble understanding that! I immediately put my hand on my rear.

Chapter Four

DECEMBER 7, 1941
THE WAR EFFORT

I'm pulling my red wagon home from a particularly good day of collecting bottles when I notice everyone's rushing out of the movies and people are crying and talking hush-hush to each other. I park my red wagon in the back hall like always and hop on each step up. to our third floor apartment. I hear Bubbie and Aunt Mayme turning the radio dial, and I know it must be something really important that's causing such a big fuss. When I get to our place, I start to say hi and my father shushes me right away. He's fooling with the aerial and the dial on the radio.

"Did you hear, Sorahlah? Did you hear? There's been a sneak attack on the United States. We picked up a New York City radio station transmitting a Honolulu reporter's statements. What a disaster. Japan has stabbed us in the back. We should get rid of all the Japs."

Mommy tries to calm him down. "Let's not jump on everybody. We need to get the information correctly. President Roosevelt is making a speech first thing tomorrow."

I sorta know who President Roosevelt is 'cause when we salute the flag, his picture is up there on the school wall along with Abraham Lincoln, Benjamin Franklin, and the handwriting chart. They're listening for more news on the radio. Dinner is sitting on the stove, but nobody seems to be in a hurry to eat. My little sister is sitting with a big bowl of cereal and a banana in her hand. Mommy shoves the same thing in front of my face.

"Eat the cereal, Sorahlah. It will hold you while we get the news. Then we will all eat together."

Daddy's been complaining about some man with a mustache named Hitler and the war in Europe for several weeks now. He says it's impossible for him to make a decent living with things so bad everywhere. His brother, Sam, offers him a job in his fur store, but Daddy doesn't want to spend the money to travel from Homewood to Squirrel Hill every day. He keeps trying to sell watches and punchboards and what Bubbie calls "cheap junk" out of his car to gas station owners and other businesspeople.

Mommy tries to explain things to me the next day after President Roosevelt speaks on the radio. "We are at war with Japan, Sorahlah. Your father's worried that he might get drafted."

"Drafted? Is that like cold air coming under the door? Bubbie complains all the time about how drafty her bedroom is. She puts newspapers all around the windows to keep the draft out."

Mommy laughs. "No, my dear child, it's a different meaning. Men will have to sign up to be in the Army or Navy and get sent to fight the war in Europe."

All this confuses me even more since I have no idea where Europe is and what it's got to do with Japan. The next week in school the teacher pulls down a map over the blackboard and shows us where Japan, Italy, and England are. She points Pennsylvania out on the map and where Pittsburgh is. It seems strange to look at a map and hear how we have to help out overseas. How would we get there? We listen to a long talk about how everyone will need to make sacrifices.

I just keep collecting bottles for my piano lessons, and then things start to change at home. Bubbie is busy putting rubber bands together in a round ball. Mommy saves every bit of silver paper from chewing gum and butter, and we start to collect and tie newspapers together. She even says that she might have to get a job to help out in a factory. My father has a fit when he hears her talk about that.

"No way, Lil. I have enough problems without you working in your condition. Forget it!"

Every time we listen to the radio, we hear how we need to buy defense bonds.

Even the teachers at school announce that each child will have a stamp book to fill up till we have $18.75, which pays for a whole bond. So now, I have to take a dime every Tuesday to school to buy a stamp and paste it in a book. I am not happy about using the money that is for my piano lessons. But Mommy says that's the sacrifice I need to make.

I worry about my birthday, which is coming on January 13, 1942. "Will I have to sacrifice that, too?"

"Your father and I promised you a birthday party, and I do not want you to sacrifice that. We've got to be careful though; everything is going to be rationed, and we will not be able make it a big party. We can manage maybe four kids." As it turns out, I end up inviting six kids. "Sorahlah, your father said only four!" She sighs and looks at my face. "OK. It isn't every day that you turn nine."

Then she tries to explain what rationing means, but I am not sure why we need to do that. She tells me and Bubbie about the notice she got in the mail to apply for sugar, gas, and other kinds of stamps that give her only a small amount of items she needs to bake a birthday cake. Bubbie clicks her false teeth and rattles off half in Yiddish mish mash to Mommy about how she knows somebody who has a way of getting stuff without a ration card.

Mommy yells at Bubbie, "That's illegal! We will do what we have to do just like everyone else."

When I collect my bottles the next week, I hear other people talking about buying at the black market without a ration card. I start to listen more carefully and figure out that the black market is what Bubbie was talking about. Why is it black? What if it spoils my birthday party? What if there's no birthday cake? Mommy won't let that happen...not my mother. I know that for sure.

The morning of the party, I can smell the cake Aunt Mayme and Mommy are baking. They won't tell me the flavor. It's supposed to be a surprise! But I think it smells like chocolate even though it must of took a whole bunch of ration stamps. Bubbie puts ice cream in her pop cooler downstairs in the candy store as a special present for me. She lets me pick out penny candy to pass out to the children who are coming. I choose wax lips, tootsie rolls and long strings of licorice—my favorite things— and wrap them in pieces of wax paper. Uncle Louie stretches twisted colored paper across the steps going up to our apartment. My cousin Sammy helps me put up a picture of a smiling donkey on our hall door for some kind of game we're gonna play. And there's a fancy wrapped package on the living room couch. Daddy says it's from Jack Gordon his friend he met hitching in California. I'm real excited. But January 13th arrives with a blizzard.

"It is snowing like hell," Daddy says. "I better go down to the cellar and stoke the furnace some more."

I hear him shovel the coal and clang the door shut. Almost right away, I can feel the hot air come up through the holes in the floor. I press my nose against the rainbow squares of the window on the door inside the vestibule. It doesn't seem to me to look like hell. More like a sparkling white bunch of pink, blue and purple sugar. Not the rationed kind. Daddy comes up the steps. His hands are black from touching the shovel and the furnace.

"Will they come to my party in the snow, Daddy?"

"Don't worry, Sorahlah. People come when they're gonna get something for free."

Then he puts his hands over the register and rubs them together. "Ah, that's better. It'll take some time though to get up to the third floor. Your mother needs to stay warm right now. She's not feeling too good with the new baby on the way."

My eyes spring open and I'm too surprised to say a word. I run up the steps two at a time. This is the best birthday present, for sure.

∽

It is a real long cold winter. When the snow piles up, Mommy makes me wear my galoshes, pulls a hat tight around my ears, and ties a red scarf across my face when I go to school. She pins my mittens to my coat even though they have a string that hangs around my neck. Somehow before March even arrives, I lose two left hands and have to wear the right hand thumb part upside down.

"I can't get you another pair, Sorahlah! You will have to let your hands freeze or put them in your pockets if you lose this pair!" my mother warns me, but I know she will never let my hands freeze. I just laugh when she says it. Then she kisses my nose, which is sticking out of the scarf, and sends me off to school. It's hard with my heavy galoshes and all my clothes on for me to make it to school on time. Everyone is dragging their feet just like me, 'cept some boys who don't even have coats on and who are making snowballs with their hands and no gloves! Their faces are red as my scarf, and I can see the breath coming out of their mouths. They don't seem to care if their hands are gonna freeze. One of the boys comes to pihahno lessons same time as me. How will he play with frozen fingers?

Then zonk! I feel a cold, hard splat against the side of my head. It practically knocks me over. Those boys are throwing snowballs at kids tryin' to walk to school. I can't yell with the scarf over my mouth, and the best I can do is walk as fast as I can, almost running to get out of their way. The snow on my hat melts running down into my eyes and I can hardly see.

The boys must be really cold. I can see them shivering, and their noses are running. Screaming and laughing, they push a small boy into a snow bank. The safety patrol boy, who is helping everyone cross at the corner, yells at them. He runs and pulls the crying kid up out of the snow. The kid looks like a big white monster. Everyone starts to laugh. *What's so funny about getting knocked over in the snow?* The boys who did it take off ahead of me for school.

By the time everyone pulls off their boots an' stuff, the cloak room is a mess of puddles and scarves and mittens. The galoshes all look alike, and I see that Mommy put a big *s* inside mine so that I can pick them out real quick. I stuff my scarf and hat inside my coat sleeve just like she told me. The boys without coats are sent to the principal's office and never come back the rest of the day. *Probably got some kind of punishment for not wearing a coat and knocking kids over. Probably got sick, too. I wonder why their mothers let them go out like that.*

Going home is even worse. The wind makes me shiver, and I slip and slide on the sidewalk. Men up on top of big trucks are throwing shovels of ashes across the road. Most of the cars have heavy chains over the tires. *It is really snowing like hell!* I surprise myself thinking something just like my father. When I get home, Mommy has some hot cocoa and a piece of buttered cinnamon toast with brown sugar. Brown sugar! How'd she get that with ration coupons? She has blue and red ones, but I don't think they are good for brown sugar. It tastes so good, I don't want to ask her.

The next day, they call off school on the radio. The snow piles up high as the back fence. I wanna go out to make a snowman. So Mommy bundles me up again with my coat and stuff, and I barely make it down the fire escape, which is full of ice.

"Hold on, Sorahlah! Try not to fall. And if you have to go to the bathroom, don't wait to the last minute."

My sister Barbara is not allowed out. She took some kind of a fit one day while we were helping Bubbie and Aunt Mayme clean cupboards. I yelled for Mommy soon as I saw her fall back. Her eyes rolled like my baby doll's. The doctor said to watch her and not let her out in the cold weather. I see her upstairs at the window waving at me and watching while I build a big snowman.

I keep piling up snow for the body. And then my cousin Sammy appears in the back yard and starts helping roll a big bunch of snow for the top. He suddenly puts a small ball together, and zonk. Just like yesterday, I get it on the side of my head. Only this time, I bend over and throw one right back in his face. He doesn't have a scarf and the snow covers his nose and mouth. But he starts licking it and laughing, and I laugh, too.

We break off sticks and give the snowman arms. Then Sam goes down behind the fire escape and comes back with a handful of coal pieces. We give our snowman coal eyes and buttons up his front and a big black ugly coal smile. Sam takes off his hat and covers the snowman's head. We are grinning just like the snowman.

"Sammy Bass, get in here right this minute. Where's your hat?" My aunt Mayme has stuck her head out of the second floor back door. Sammy's sister Marilyn is staring out the window, and above her face, my sister Barbara is staring out of our third-floor window. I am standing with the snow up to my knees. Sammy goes inside. My mother has not called me in. I continue to pat the snowman's tummy, making it round and full. The sky is gray, and it is getting colder again.

Then I feel that urge! *Oh, my.* I have trouble getting my feet up out of the deep snow. The fire escape is really *slippy.* I hold on to the rails with mittens soaking with snow. *Hurry up! Hurry up!* I finally make it to the back door and my mother opens it. My legs feel wet and warm. She looks at my face and at the snow covering half my leggings and coat. She immediately knows.

"I couldn't make it in time, Mommy." She says nothing.

My mother takes off my coat and leggings and hangs them to dry on a chair over the register where the heat is pouring out. She puts my hat and scarf and my mittens in front of the oven, which is on to keep the kitchen warmer. Then she strips my other clothes off and wraps me in a towel. She fills the bathtub with warm water and throws in some bubble powder. I soak and feel my body getting warm again. I think about how cold and lost those boys must be with no mother to make them wear coats and put them in a warm bath.

Then I hear the oven racks squeaking as my mother pulls out the broiler pan. Soon, I can smell the cinnamon and brown sugar and know that there will be hot sweet toast and cocoa in a big cup.

༄

Spring comes and the backyard starts to look altogether different. The forsythia along the fence is full of yellow blooms. I can see the berry vines are starting to get leaves. The weeds are coming up in clumps and there is a robin who visits every morning. My Uncle Louie, Aunt Mayme's husband, is back from one of his long trips working on putting plumbing into big skyscrapers. He's using Bubbie's garage to store his tools. You can always hear him clanging pipes and can see the light bulb swinging through the window, which has lost one of its panes during the snowstorm. I like watching him work putting pipes together with a fire that comes out of what he calls a torch. He shows me all his tools and lets me hold down large pipes while he saws them. Sometimes he even lets me hand him the right screwdriver or hammer. He tells me our cousin Hymie has a scrap yard and how everyone is saving metal to get it melted down and turned into things the country needs for the war effort. "I sell scrap metal I get from jobs to make extra bucks." He describes to Sammy and me all the places he's been besides New Jersey where he's from and how he's worked on famous building projects high in the air. "I walk 'cross dem big steel beams like nut-tin'," he exclaims. "I'm expert at puttin' in toilets."

Right now, Uncle Louie is helping dig up the yard instead of paying Bubbie the garage rent. Bubbie, Mommy and Mayme, are getting ready to put in *a victory garden.* The government is giving out seeds and instructions on how to plant your own vegetables. We are going to have beans, tomatoes, onions, cucumbers and carrots and lots of herbs. Everyone is planting a victory garden. The nuns in Holy Rosary Church are busy digging; the church school is offering space on property they own to people who don't have a yard. Even Grandma and Aunt Elaine in Squirrel Hill are putting in plants.

We follow the instructions that come with the seeds very care-fully. Every day when I come home from school, I check to see if the seeds are sprouting. I have the job of watering the garden and checking for weeds and pulling them out. Mommy's got a big round belly and can't do any bending in the garden. We talk a lot about how to put up tomatoes and pickles and beans in jars for the winter.

Now when I take my red wagon and go on an endless hunt for bottles, it's harder than it used to be before the war just like my father says. "People want to turn in their own bottles and keep the two cents or the nickels." Bubbie tells me everyone's tight with a dollar. My father says, "No one could be as tight as she is." My mother and father are constantly arguing about paying the rent to Bubbie who's always mad at Mommy for not making my father pay her first.

"For two cents, I'd move out of here in a minute." My father's arguing with Mommy.

"Well, it'll take a lot more than two cents to move and your income is not enough to support us totally. We're lucky my mother looks the other way about the rent." It goes on like that for a while and then Mommy's back goes out and Daddy quits his hollering.

As for me, I'm savin' money to buy my own piano. I keep hoping that the clackity one at Uncle Abe's auction place will be there when I get enough saved up. Even my two birthday quarters from my grandma in Squirrel Hill are still under my bed in a shiny box with roses painted on it. And Miss Allison, who's real nice about letting me practice at school, tells me not to worry about the twenty-five cents either. But I don't think it'll ever be enough! One thing for sure, my 'rithmetic improves from counting.

But even more exciting, when it's almost the end of June, Mommy tells me I'll be going to Emma Kaufmann summer camp in Harmony, Pa. "Two whole weeks, Sorahlah! You'll be going in the middle of August all the way to Zelienople out in the country," she exclaims giving me a hug.

"But the money?" I almost shout thinking about my saved up money under my bed. "I don't have enough..."

She quickly interrupts, "I got you a scholarship! That means we will not have to pay."

By the end of July, Mommy and Aunt Mayme are busily sewing my name in my clothes and on some towels and sheets while I'm busily pulling weeds out of the garden thinking about my first overnight camping trip. A terrible thought occurs to me: we have to go all the way to Zelienople and then to Harmony on a bus to get there! How could I've forgot about my big problem with car trips? I get carsick! What if I get bus sick? *I can't get sick!* I keep telling myself: *I will not get sick.*

Then there's Mommy and the new baby. "Mommy, who'll help you with the garden? And what if the baby comes before I get home?"

"Oh, my dear little sweet Sorahlah. Everything will be fine. As for the baby, don't worry! I'll wait for you to come home."

Chapter Five

ONLY IF IT FITS
AUGUST 1942

All during July and the beginning of August, I look around every Saturday at Uncle Abe's auction for the old piano; it's still on the stage. Then one weekend, it isn't! I about bust out crying. But Daddy gives me his you-know-what look. Then after school, two weeks before I leave for my camp vacation, I see Mommy standing across the street in front of the movie house, looking up at our high windows. "Just be very careful! This piano means a lot to my child." Her voice is sorta shaky.

"No one knows better than us, missus. Uncle Abe says it's a good ole upright. Just right for Sorahlah." The big black piano guy digs his feet into the ground and holds onto the ropes. I almost scream but clap my hand on my mouth. My eyes bulge. I can't even breathe. Bubbie stands looking up, too, her hand over her eyes like she's saluting the American flag. "*Du needst dat ting vie uh loch in kop.* Better my rent den diss." She goes into the candy store mumbling, pulls down the blind on the door and puts a closed sign in the side window. The sun blinds my eyes. I try my bubbie's salute. I'm almost crazy with curiosity. And then wow! Up in the air—hanging with a big grey quilt and lots of ropes, all covered up except for the gold pedals—swinging—swinging...

"My husband got it for just five dollars. He's really proud Sorahlah could help out with the money. She's been saving for months and months. Please hurry. I want it to be in place before Sorahlah gets home from school. She's going to be so surprised. But be careful."

"Real careful, missus."

I jump out at Mommy. I can't stay still another minute. "I see Uncle Abe's moving guys. Did Daddy's new chair come?" I feel proud fooling Mommy about the surprise. She grabs her big belly with both hands and lets out a loud bunch of air from her mouth.

"Sorahlah, you really scared me. It's something much more important. A surprise!"

"A surprise? Is it for the new baby, something for the new baby? A big girl bed for my sister?" I can hardly keep from laughing and pretending I don't know.

"You can't guess this one. It's for my sweet child, my little Sorahlah."

I grab Mommy's big belly and bury my face in her dress. I'm afraid to look at the moving guys holding the long ropes.

"Okie dokie, Joe, now don't swing the rope, just pull it. Ready? On a count of one-two-hoist!"

"Mommy, Mommy, the old—pyeano—oops—pihahno—from Uncle Abe's auction. What's it doing here? Is it for me?" She kisses my head and then my nose. "For me, for me—a real piano. Mommy, my own dear mommy." I know that there's been a lot of yelling and throwing of dishes over Mommy never having enough money for the rent. But then Daddy feels happy knowing he's getting the chair he wants, and today there it is: the big clackity swinging on ropes high in the air.

"Now you can really practice. But only when Daddy's not home or your little sister isn't sleeping."

"Will it wake the baby sleeping in your tummy?" We both laugh at my silliness. I hop from one foot to the other. "Why's it in the air? It's going to fall! What if it falls?"

"A few more pulls, Joe." They grunt and pull. "Careful, careful. Don't give it no slack. Don't worry, little Sorahlah. We'll get your piano up there through the fire escape in good shape." Water runs down their faces as they huff and puff and pull.

"Miss Allison will be so pleased. But there's only one more lesson and…"

"Don't get excited. You'll have plenty of lessons when school starts again in September. And besides, you'll be away for two weeks at camp. You can pick out all the songs you like from the radio till then and practice in your new blue book. Be careful when you set it in the living room, Joe. Don't scratch the floor, please."

"Watch! Watch! Be careful of my pihahno." *I sound just like Miss Allison.* I dance around, pulling at my mother's dress and almost unwrapping the tie on the skirt. Mommy laughs.

∽

The day I leave for camp my tummy's full of butterflies. *Don't get car sick—don't get car sick! It's all I can think about.* My father puts my suitcase and duffle-bag into the big pile next to the busses standing ready. A woman is arguing with the driver who's checking all the bags. I can hear the bus driver yelling, "Only two, Missus! Only two…" The woman yells back at him, "You can make it fit. That family only has one large duffle." My mother who read the instructions very carefully shakes her head. "Some people don't want to follow the rules. "My father adds, "If everybody brings more than the two bags the bus'll be overloaded and unsafe. It doesn't matter if it fits or not!" Before I know it I'm in a seat next to an open window waving 'bye to Mommy who is smiling and holding on to Daddy's arm. I can see her belly is really getting big. "Wait for me to come home, Mommy!" I holler out the window. But she can't hear me over the counselors who are singing "*Over-hill over-dale as we hit the dusty trail and the caissons go rolling along…*" and shouting out names off a list. Soon everyone is singing and clapping and having a noisy good time. *So far so good…I am not sick.*

When we unload at camp a big truck takes all the bags up the hill. I'm in the "Redbird" cabin. I get to hang my towel in a little wooden cubby and put my toothbrush and powder on the shelf. My suitcase fits under the cot and my duffle's at the end of the bed. The counselor shows us how to make up our beds with hospital corners and how to stuff the pillow in the case. I smile 'cause my mother who studied nursing showed me how to do that on my own bed at home. I help the girl in the next bed do her corners just right and she thanks me. Just when I'm putting my pajamas under the pillow, a loud bell rings and we have to line up to go to the dining hall for lunch.

Lunch is macaroni and cheese or peanut butter and grape jelly or plain cheese sandwiches on white bread. There's big bowls of applesauce along with sweating cold pitchers of milk on each table. I choose chocolate milk and a peanut butter and jelly sandwich even though the sandwich sticks to the roof of my mouth and I gag trying to get it loose with my finger. *I suddenly realize I never got sick on the trip!* After lunch we get a tour of the campgrounds and each cabin hears what the schedule will be for the first week. "No swimming today but perhaps tomorrow, "the counselor says. "Today we are going to play a game and learn everybody's name and then you all need to rest before dinner! It's a special treat tonight—spaghetti with meat sauce." By the time I finish unpacking clothes after dinner and brush my teeth, I'm ready for bed. But it seems the bed is not ready for me. I feel like *The Princess and the Pea* story—every spring and wire digs into my side. How'll I survive this torture? The next thing I know the camp bell is clanging and it's morning.

Camp's OK except I am not happy with waking up when it's still dark. I have to brush my teeth and wash with freezing water. My skin shivers with little goose bumps till I get my clothes on. Our counselor makes us fix up our beds and hang up our clothes. She inspects the beds and us, and insists everybody's hair's brushed and shoes are tied and hurries us outside. We all have to line up while the American flag is raised and say the *Pledge of Allegiance.* Then everyone rushes to the dining room for breakfast, which is OK with me. I love cooked oatmeal! No limits on the sugar and raisins I can put in and there's plenty of buttered toast with apple butter. *I don't know how they get enough ration stamps.* Some of the girls who are from East Liberty or Squirrel Hill know each other and sit together and laugh and chatter. I'm the only girl who's from Homewood-Brushton in my cabin. My cousin Zelda's kids who are in an older group sit on the other side of the dining room. They wave at me when we pass. But except for the girl who sleeps in the cot next to me, I don't really talk much to anyone.

After breakfast each day we get to do all kinds of activities. I spend the first three days learning how to make a lanyard: a twisted red, white and blue bracelet that's like leather just for my mommy. When that's done, I spend two days decorating a folded piece of paper with crayons and paint for my little sister's birthday on September 2nd, which will be right after I get home. My tummy gets sudden butterflies! What if the baby comes on Barbara Lea's birthday? She'd get cheated of her own day! I decide to make her a wood cut-out of her own name along with the card. I hardly get the card finished when it's already day seven at camp, and my cabin has to take a turn doing physical exercise before lunch so I never get to trace on the wood. I wear the lanyard on my hand from then on and put the card at the bottom of my suitcase.

At the end of the first week, the head of the camp announces at lunch, "There are fresh vegetables and cheeses from the local farm up the road on each table. We are planning a field trip to the farm to see how the farmer milks the cows and grows his garden." Everyone is excited to hear about this extra trip. There are big platters on the tables with slices of bright red tomatoes, cucumbers and green pepper chunks along with pieces of yellow, white and funny looking cheese with holes in it. Then I see one counselor piling up the tomatoes and cucumbers with lots of salt on two pieces of bread. *Wow! She's making a sandwich that reminds me of the time I learned to read at the library.* I make a big tomato sandwich and add the cheese with holes. It hardly fits into my mouth. When I bite down, the juicy tomatoes squeeze out the sides of the bread and land on my clean shirt. But oh what a treat! This cheese tastes different— not at all like the American cheese they serve every other day. I hope the farmer will bring his fresh vegetables again soon.

After lunch we go to our cabin where we get our mail call and have to write a card to our mother and father. After the first four days in camp, I get three postcards all at once from Mommy with news about the garden and Daddy and Barbara Lea. Then we are supposed to take a nap. The girls who sit together at lunch usually sneak over to each other's cots and whisper and giggle until the counselor yells at them. The girl next to me actually takes a nap snoring as loud as my bubbie.

Rest time drags. But in the afternoon, most of the camp activities are hot and noisy except for the nature hike. When my cabin takes its hike, I love tramping through the woods. We spot a deer and bunnies and learn about bird watching and how to identify poison ivy from other plants. It sure is different than going to the zoo. I have lots to write on my post-card especially since I passed my swimming test. We can also choose from painting lessons, group races, baseball, and volleyball. Bad choice for me! I twist my ankle playing volleyball. The counselor says, "Choose another activity without running or jumping." When I request a music lesson, she sends me to the music cabin, but there's no teacher. Instead, I play recordings on an old phonograph. My favorite is a *something in Blue*. I can hardly wait to try to do it on my new piano. The one in the music cabin has no sound in the middle and all the white keys are broken or missing. With my hobbling foot, I miss the next day's trip to the farmer, but I go to the music cabin and read a book about Mozart while I listen to recordings. Even though I'm by myself, I enjoy the coolness and the quiet.

Everyone's back from the trip by dinnertime. But this dinner's not for me. It's thick stew or mashed potatoes with meatloaf, hotdogs with sauerkraut or baked beans. No fresh tomatoes from the farmer and not even any peanut butter and grape jelly. I was hoping for spaghetti again, but no such luck. I take my chances with the hotdogs and kraut, but not the stew, which has fatty pieces I can't chew. On the Fridays we are there, we get sliced *chaloh* with our meal, but there is only one piece for each kid. There's no milk at dinner since this is a kosher camp. I know there'll be a bedtime snack, so I don't much care.

Most evenings after dinner we sit around outside and tell ghost stories or sing camp songs till it's time to lower the American flag. If it's raining, the counselors let us fool around with five-hundred piece puzzles, playing checkers, "Old Maid" or reading in the cabin. One bright cool night the "Redbirds" get their turn to go into the woods and make a campfire in a big clearing. Everyone gathers wood and the counselor shows us how to build a pyramid and light the fire with rolled up newspaper. Then we all have to find a good long stick and poke a marshmallow onto its end. We carefully toast it in the flames. Some girls burn their marshmallows or drop them in the fire. Lucky for me I get to taste the gooey treat even though it burns my tongue.

Best of all, I learn two new songs: *Kookaburra sits in the old gum tree,* and one that makes me get goose bumps—*White Coral Bells.* We sing both songs in what they call a round—taking turns starting the song at different times. I enjoy hearing the voices singing different words and making the music have what Miss Allison once told me is harmony. Then we stand in a circle and link arms while we finish up with a song we learned another night: *There's a Long, Long Trail A Winding.* The smell of the woods, the sound of the campfire crackling and the firelight on all the singing faces makes me want camping to go on and on forever. That night I fall asleep and can feel my face smiling.

On the very last night at camp after we've packed all our dirty clothes up and put the duffle bags and suitcases at the foot of our cots, we go outside and wait for the flag to be lowered. Then we sit on the grass in a circle, and the counselor lights a candle in the middle of the circle. I can see all the other cabins are doing the same thing. I can hear squeaking and see the kitchen servers wheeling carts across the grass. They pass out what the head cook calls *s'mores*: graham crackers with chocolate syrup and melted marshmallows from the kitchen oven. We each get a little box of milk with it for our evening snack. While we eat and lick the chocolate off our fingers, we take turns talking about something special at home. I decide to read aloud from my mother's last post-card, which is in my sweater pocket. I tell the girls in a soft voice, "Every postcard from my mother talks about the new baby almost ready to be born in our family." I am surprised when the girls all sigh and laugh. They are actually pleased to listen. I continue much louder. "My mother writes: soon—as you get home—I'm waiting for you." Everyone applauds and I get a hug from the girl sitting next to me. After that, it makes me feel happy to hear everyone tell her story. I applaud them just as they applauded me. Then we all stand, link arms and sing *White Coral Bells* just like we did around the campfire—swaying back and forth. I can hear the voices across the whole camp. How my ears ring with that sound! I can hardly wait to tell Mommy about my camping experience. She'll be so proud of how grownup I've become in camp. But mostly, I can hardly wait to hold the new baby.

⌒

Then, finally, I'm coming back on the bus. It takes forever. But as it turns out, I do not get bus sick coming back. There's all the people waiting outside the YMHA. I don't see anyone for me 'cept Cousin Zelda waiting for her kids. "Where's my mother? Is my father here?" Zelda doesn't answer. She's too busy yelling at her kids. She piles me, my suitcase and laundry bag into the back of her car. Her kids are fighting already. She just keeps yelling. I squeeze my eyes shut so I won't get carsick in the back of the car. I jump out at home and run up the three flights bumping my dirty laundry bag behind me. Zelda brings up the suitcase to my father standing at the top of the third floor door. They don't even say hello. He's in his undershirt and his suspenders hang down his pants. Zelda hurries back down the stairs.

"Daddy, Daddy. Where's Mommy? She wasn't at the bus. Is the new baby here? Is it a boy or a girl? Are they in the hostibul?"

"Sorah, I'm sorry to have to tell you but…it's just one of those things. It happens." My father is awful red in the face.

"*Meina tochter…meina… Got—oy yoy, yoy—meina tochter.*" Bubbie's screaming from downstairs makes him turn away from me. I cover my ears.

Daddy hollers louder than I ever heard him yell at Mommy. "Stop that screaming about your daughter. I can't hear myself think." he yells down the steps and bangs the door closed. It doesn't help much. Her screams keep on and on.

"What's wrong with Bubbie? Is she sick? Why is she crying? Where's Mommy? Where's my sister? Where's the new baby?"

"Your mother isn't coming home. The baby is with her." He is talking up to the air. He puts on his shirt buttoned all wrong.

"But Mommy promised me I could help with the baby. She promised. When will they be home?"

"She died."

"Died? What does that mean?"

"She will never be back...no, never!"

"What do you mean? I have a card from her the last day in camp. She says the baby's almost ready to be born. She's waiting for me. Where's the baby? Where is my mother?"

"She died with the baby." I can hardly hear his voice. He snaps his suspenders in place and buttons his cuffs.

"Huh? Died with the baby? Is the baby a boy or girl?"

"The baby was another girl."

"But where's the little girl?"

"They both died. The funeral is tomorrow. Now pack your suitcase." He puts it on my bed.

"Why do I have to pack? I just got home from camp. Mommy has to help me. My clothes are all dirty. I want to wait for Mommy."

"Do as I say. Take enough clothes for one week. You'll be with Grandma. Your sister's already there."

"Grandma? Will Mommy be there with us?"

"No! How many times do I have to say it?" I have no trouble hearing that.

"I don' wanna go."

"Tomorrow is the funeral. You don't have a choice."

"A funeral? Is it that place up the street?"

"Jews don't bury their dead there. That's for the *goyem*."

"But where will Mommy be?"

"Your mother is not coming back. She's never coming back. She is dead. You will go to live with your grandmother. We'll need to move out of here. I won't be able to take care of you two by myself. My mother will take us in." His voice is hoarse, shaking. He takes a tie off the doorknob and puts it under his shirt collar.

"Why can't we stay here in our own rooms? Bubbie can take care of us."

"I would not stay with that cheap old witch! I don't want her anywhere near me. Now, get going. Pack. I have too much to worry about."

"But I don't know how to pack. How'll I pack my piano? We need to call Uncle Abe and the movers…"

"Damn that piano. I will not spend money on it anymore. Bring only your clothes. Nothing else, do you hear me? Now get ready. Pick out a good dress for the funeral. I want you to look presentable."

"Can I take my red wagon with me?"

"What? Didn't you hear me? Go pack now!"

"My red wagon—I need to take it with me."

"Only if it fits in the car. Now hurry up. Your grandmother's waiting."

I put my book of pomes and the red and blue piano books in the bottom of the suitcase on top of my sister's birthday card. I reach under my bed and take out my moneybox. It looks just like the same amount before my real piano came. I rub the lanyard on my wrist, sigh and dump all my nickels, dimes and quarters into an old winter knee sock without even counting.

Bubbie's screaming gets louder. "*Meina tochter…yoy, yoy!*"

I cover my ears.

Chapter Six

THE FUNERAL
AUGUST 1942

When Daddy and I get to Grandma's, everyone's in the kitchen talking about food for after the funeral. It seems it's gonna be like a party or something. Daddy puts my suitcase at the bottom of the steps. I'm looking down at my shoes. Grandma rushes out and gives me a big hug, which nearly knocks me over. My stomach's making funny noises, and Grandma pulls me into the kitchen.

"Avraham, did Sorahlah *ge gessen?*"

My father shrugs his shoulders, slumps in a chair, and buries his head in his hands. He's awful quiet for my father.

Grandma repeats herself to me. "Did you eat something, Sorahlah?" Suddenly, my stomach makes a real funny noise. "Ach!" Grandma shakes her head. She takes out a bottle of milk and cuts me a big piece of honey cake. I'm real surprised to get cake for dinner. It tastes sweet and sticky and I lick my fingers real quick, but nobody seems to notice what I'm doing. They're all busy speaking Hungarian too fast for me to understand. My feet swing under the table and soon my eyes begin to feel real sleepy.

My Aunt Elaine—Daddy's sister—takes me by the hand and, half hugging me, leads me up the steps. She takes off my shorts and white camp shirt. She wipes my face and hands with a cool washrag and hugs me again. All this hugging is really getting me nervous. She takes off my gum bands, and runs her fingers through my hair.

"Oy, yoy, yoy—you need a bath and a good shampoo, too. Tomorrow morning first thing!" She tiptoes into the bedroom, motioning me after her. My little sister, who's just gonna be five, is already sleeping in the bed on the side by the wall. I can see her eyes closed like petal cups on a flower. She breathes real easy like my mommy says the new baby is practicing inside her tummy.

"Where's my own bed?" I sound real whiney. "And I don't have my jammies."

But Aunt Elaine just picks me up and lays me down. She gives me a real smooshy kiss. Her black hair is in rollers and her hands smell of Lady Esther hand cream—the same kind my mother uses. She has on a housedress and bedroom slippers. But you can still see her "wonderful figure," as Mommy always says about her sister-in-law. They're good friends.

"Tomorrow is the funeral. You know that, Sorahlah?"

I nod but still do not quite understand. "Will Mommy be there?" Aunt Elaine turns and rushes out of the room. She leaves the hall light on and the door open. Downstairs, I hear the Hungarian getting louder and I hear Grandma starting to cry.

The next thing I know, it's morning and a strange lady is shaking me awake. "Come on now, Shirley, you need to get up and get ready." My eyes blink open.

My sister's not in the bed. Everyone is rushing around. I can hear my bubbie's voice crying again and again, "*Meina tochter... oy...meina tochter.*"

My father is yelling just like he did before, "Quit your cryin'! Yuh never cared about your daughter before. Why now?"

Why is Bubbie here?

The lady who waked me up is very tall with shiny blond hair that looks like wavy glue on her head. She throws back the covers and sits on the edge of the bed. "Do you understand what a funeral is?" She keeps right on talking. "When somebody dies they need to be buried in the ground and they are in a casket and then everyone says good-bye to them. That's what will happen today to your mother. You must get up and ready to go. My name is Helen, and I'm your Uncle Sam's wife. I'm supposed to help you get dressed." Then she takes my hand and pulls me into the bathroom, fills the bathtub with water, and hands me a bar of soap and a washrag. "Wash real hard and scrub your hair, too. I'll come in and check you to make sure you did a good job."

I really don't believe Mommy would leave me or that I have to say good-bye to her. And besides, she has to come in and rinse my hair for me and help me dry off real good so I don't get chapped. I don't like that this Helene person's gonna do what my mother does. But I wash real quick when she starts banging on the door telling me other people have to use the bathroom. I dunk my head under the water and climb over the tub and hardly wrap the towel around myself when she yanks me into the bedroom, dries me only halfway, and tells me to dress myself. She has put my blue dress with the little collar and tieback on the bed along with underwear and socks and my buckle shoes. The dress is sticking to my wet back and my hair's dripping. Then she takes a comb to my hair and has it braided and fixed with two gum bands before I can say ouch or ooh.

I look at her real good up close. This is the first time I've seen this person, although I heard my mother and father talking about how pretty Sam's new wife is. Her lips shaped like a bow are pink and her eyelashes have lots of black stuff on them just like Aunt Elaine's. She is tall and thin like Uncle Sam 'cept he has black slicked-back hair and a mustache. He always wears a fancy looking suit with a vest and a chain hanging from the front of it. I don't like him 'cause he always calls me toothpick and tries to pinch my nose or yank my braids. Mommy thinks he pretends like he's a movie star named Erley Flynn or something like that. *One thing is certain, Helene smells of some kinda flower I can't name. Whew!*

"Helene, will you take me and my sister to the funeral?"

"My name's Helen, honey, not Helene. Your father will take you. That's his job, not mine. Your sister's too little to go to a funeral."

And with that she hurries me down the steps past my bubbie, who is still crying, and my father, who keeps putting his head in his hands. My aunt Elaine's hair is curled up on top of her head and she is putting on her eye makeup looking in a tiny mirror and making her eyes roll back and blink a lot. She always says she wouldn't be caught dead with her face all naked. Helen pulls me into the kitchen where Grandma pours out milk on a dish of corn-flakes for me to eat. Grandma ties a dishtowel 'round my neck to keep my dress clean. Helen goes out on the back porch, banging the door shut. I can see the smoke from her cigarette filling up the window over the sink.

Eva, my grandma's maid, who always comes to clean and iron and whatever else Grandma needs, is pushing the carpet sweeper. I like her 'cause she isn't much bigger than me and always talks to me when I get left at Grandma's for the weekend. But today Grandma's telling her about what to put on the table in time for everybody to eat and how there has to be a pitcher with water and a cup and a towel on the front porch for everyone to wash their hands when they come back from the cemetery. *Cemetery? What are we going there for?* Eva just nods and comes over to me. "I real sorry 'bout yur mudder, kiddo." And she pats my hand. Washing hands outside on the porch? Sorry about my mother? Suddenly the cereal is mush and my stomach feels sick.

Grandma puts a hat on her head. She has on a black dress she only wears for the holidays. Aunt Elaine has a black dress on, too, and fixes a black veil with pimples on it over her face. My bubbie has on an old coat and a straw hat and holds her purse real tight. Then I see somebody sitting on Grandpa's big chair. *Is it my mother?* But she has curls all over the top of her head and a black dress on with flowers painted on it. I squint my eyes and see it's my aunt Mayme, Mommy's sister. *Bubbie and Aunt Mayme never ever come to Grandma and Grandpa's house. Where's Grandpa? Where's Uncle Sam?*

Daddy gets up and announces that the car has arrived. It's a long black shiny car with a man in a funny looking hat driving. "Into the car, Sorahlah. You sit in the middle. Mayme, you and your mother can ride in the back with Elaine and my mother. I'll ride up front with the driver."

Helen gets into her own car—cigarette hanging from her pink mouth. Eva is setting up a pitcher of water and a towel on the porch. I start counting to keep myself from getting carsick. I can't get this dress dirty before the funeral. I say this word inside my head again and again—*funeral, funeral, funeral!* No one says anything the whole way. Everyone 'cept me has a hanky. Grandma keeps dabbing at her eyes. Aunt Elaine holds hers in her hand. Bubbie's is crumpled up like paper around her purse handle.

And then we're there and get out and go into the "chapel," the driver calls it. *A chapel? I thought only Holy Rosary Church had a chapel. I guess funerals need them, too.* Nobody pays attention to me so I just stand outside the big wood doors. But then Daddy pushes one side open and grabs my hand and starts pulling me to the front of a whole bunch of rows with people already seated and busy talking. I can see Grandpa and Uncle Sam sitting in a little room with their yarmulkes on, and Grandpa has his *tallis* around his shoulders and is reading from his black *siddur*. Bubbie and Aunt Mayme sit down on chairs across from him. Bubbie just stares at the floor, but she's not crying anymore. Aunt Mayme's lips are moving; I can't tell if she is talking or what.

Daddy pulls me up to a long shiny box. He whispers, "Look, Sorahlah, she looks just like she's sleeping!" I gape 'cause there she is—my mommy—all dressed up in her best clothes. Her hair combed and curled and her hands folded over her chest. She has rouge on her face and is so still. *How can this be?*

"Touch her, Sorahlah—so you can say good-bye." My father grabs my hand. I feel frozen and sweaty. He makes me stroke my mother's hair. My throat is choking. My heart beats so hard I can hear it inside the front of my eyes. For one minute, I see her eyes open and look at me and her lips move. I pull away from my father.

"Kiss your mother, Shirley...say good-bye." Daddy yanks me nearer the box and tries to push my head down. I jerk away and run and hide my face in Grandpa's jacket. He holds my shaking hand in his big fist and speaks in Hungarian, which I can't understand.

Uncle Sam tells me, "He says he will take care of you since you no longer have a mother."

Since I no longer have a mother! I no longer have a mother. I no longer have a mother. I bite my tongue and cover my mouth with my hand to keep from yelping like a dog. Bubbie is awful quiet, but Aunt Mayme is gulping and choking and crying at the same time. Grandma and Aunt Elaine shake their heads. Grandma's chewing her handkerchief. Aunt Elaine lifts her veil and dabs her cheeks.

Uncle Sam goes to meet Helen who is walking down the aisle. I see him try to pinch her arm. She smacks his hand so hard everyone in the place turns around and looks at them. She goes right up to the long box and looks at my mother. I keep seeing Mommy's eyes staring at me.

Then I climb up on Grandpa's lap and whisper in his ear. "Grandpa, where is the new little baby sister from Mommy's tummy?"

"They put her at your mother's feet in the bottom of the casket."

I try real hard not to cry.

Chapter Seven

PAPRIKASH
EARLY SPRING 1943

Life at Grandma's for sure is different. But some things I can count on every week like getting ready for school, helping Grandma set the table, and running the mangle to press the sheets. But always, the arguing! The arguing really hurts my ears. My daddy hollers at my Uncle Sam, my Aunt Elaine hollers at my father, and they all holler at Grandma. They argue about everything and anything 'cept one thing: what's for dinner? It seems that they could argue and lift the pot lid and taste the soup or smack their lips on a potato and continue hollering. This goes on all the time 'cept when Grandpa's home. Then Grandma shushes us. "*Shah, shtill! Apoukah* is sleeping!" Or *dahven*ing or singing or preparing for the *Shabbes* services.

Everyone tiptoes around when Grandpa is at home. He demands total quiet and immediate obedience. Me included! When he gets mad, his chest puffs up; his white beard trembles and his blue eyes bulge with anger. He seems like a giant when he's angry. His face is red and his voice gets louder when dinner isn't ready or Grandma runs out of money before payday. As for me, he really gets mad when I stand behind him weaving and bobbing while he practices singing for services. I almost can't help myself and start to sing along.

He hollers at Grandma. "*Onyoukah*, she's doing it again! No singing allowed from the women. Do you hear me, Sorahlah?" He spits and sputters and continues muttering into his black prayer book.

Grandma yanks me into the kitchen. "*Dahven*ing like that is not allowed for a girl." And she sets me to work stirring the pots or

drying the dishes. But I copy Grandpa anyway when no one's look-
ing. I take his black prayer book—the *siddur*—and try to read the
Hebrew and sing the prayers, which I'm pretty good at. Of course,
I get caught again and again.

Some times the arguing and hollering is about Daddy's girlfriend, Thelma, whom nobody seems to like. Uncle Sam makes
fun of her "bazoomas"—he calls them—using his hands out in
front of him, and then adds, "And she's taller and a good foot
wider than you, little brother. In bed, she'll sound like a whoopee
cushion." That about drives Grandma crazy. I guess a whoopee
cushion is something dirty or ugly.

This remark really sets my father off. "You blow all your bucks
on women off the street, you phony. I'm gonna move out of this
dump as soon as I save some cash. At least I plan to get married.
You're a real leech."

But the loudest arguing is about the constant gin games Daddy
plays with Uncle Sam. Uncle Sam keeps a careful running total, he
calls it, on how much Daddy owes. Daddy keeps the same thing on
his brother.

"You owe me, you cheapskate," is Daddy's favorite insult.

"Set the date for Sunday, after dinner! We'll see who's the winner!"

When they aren't picking on each other or Grandma, they torture my aunt Elaine. And when their insults of her get used up,
I'm it. My clothes, my hair, my posture, and what Uncle Sam calls
my constant whiny voice. Then there's who's gonna pay for my
clothes or take me to the doctor's, or you name it. One thing for
sure, Daddy is not interested in what's happening in my life or at
school.

"I can't go to the school for the *what-a-yah call it*—teacher talk,
Sorahlah."

"Conference, brother mine—it's called a conference," Aunt
Elaine hollers.

"Shut up, you budinsky. Who asked you anyway?"

"Avraham! Show respect in this house. *Ne szemtelenkedz.*" Grandma
gets in Daddy's face. I know what that means in Hungarian. "Don't

use that kind of language!" Grandma is always telling Daddy and Uncle Sam that.

"I'll use whatever damn language I want. I pay you enough for what little I'm here." Daddy's blue eyes bulge just like Grandpa's.

Then Uncle Sam has to get in his hollering, too. "When is it you are ever here? And you added up wrong in the last gin game! Pay up." Then he turns on my aunt. "Sister, dear, too much makeup, sweetheart. You look like a French *hoor.*"

My aunt's face darkens. "Sam! Not in front of the child, you…"

"That ugly skinny toothpick. She's a dummy and a *nahr.*" My Uncle Sam laughs in a way that makes me want to holler, too. I'm trying real hard not to cry! Grandma's stirring the pot furiously. My aunt jumps in to save me.

"Don't call her a fool. You are the fool and nothing but a skirt chaser. No wonder your wife walked out on you."

"Yeah! And where's that greenhorn husband of yours? Sure, sure— learning to be a baker up in Detroit or somewhere. Fat chance."

I can see my aunt is close to tears. "You're a real pig, you know that?"

Grandma joins the hollering. "Don't use that *trayfe* word!" Grandma does not approve of using the p-i-g word.

"Never mind, little Shirley. You are going to be gorgeous." Aunt Elaine pats my head. I know she cares about me 'cause she got me a real big doll for my birthday, special ribbons for my hair, and she shows me how to pinch my cheeks to make my white skin have color. Uncle Sam and Daddy are real angry with my aunt all the time, 'specially since Grandma let her move in on the third floor while her husband is getting work in Detroit. They all stay on the third floor. But I don't think Aunt Elaine has to pay.

"You dress like a hussy, too. All those fancy schmancy clothes from Frank & Seder."

Daddy joins in. "They look like they come from the basement."

"Lower basement, you mean. Oh, hey, Essie, you've got a run!" Uncle Sam sneers at her.

My aunt looks quickly down at her legs. "Oh, god, not again!"

"For *shamet zee*! Don't use the name of the Lord!" Grandma is against the G-d word, too.

My aunt realizes there's no run in her stocking. "Idiot! You're just jealous, both of you, 'cause I get an employee discount."

Grandma chimes in. "Elonka, don't forget to layaway that new coat for Sor. She's too big for her old one."

My father suddenly sweetens his tone. "Better get me some new shirts and that pair of brown and white shoes first. I need to look good for my customers."

"To hell with your customers! Where's my money? You owe me first." My uncle suddenly pulls a pad off the telephone table and sticks it in Daddy's face. Uncle Sam's voice gets louder. "Pay up!"

"My dear brother Sam, that's because you cheat when you add up. Yuh can't add." Daddy rips the paper off the tablet, crumples it and throws it in Sam's face.

"He can't add? Look who's talkin'. Yuh owe me, too, my dear little brother Aaron." My aunt folds her arms and taps her foot in disgust. "He's too busy with his lady friend, *shpatszeering* all over town."

Grandma rattles off her own really fast mish mash of Hungarian mixed with Yiddish while she hits the pot with her wooden spoon. Then the phone rings.

"Sorahlah, answer the phone. Sorahlah! Do you hear me?" Grandma shouts at the back of my head as I go out onto the porch and plop into a wicker rocker.

"Why? It's not *Shabbes* !" I am supposed to answer the phone only on Friday night and Saturday. Grandma says I am her *Shabbes Goy*!

Uncle Sam gets the phone instead. "Shut up all of you! I can't hear a thing." He shouts into the receiver. "Hello, what? Who? Oh, him. Is there someone here called Aaron?"

My father grabs the phone. Sam slaps him on the head. "Your girlfriend, huh, Romeo? Try that for a name." My father does not like to be called Avraham or even Aaron. He wants to change his name to something he thinks is more American. I can hear Grandma mumbling furiously in Hungarian.

My father purrs into the phone "Oh, hi, Thel. Yeah! I'll get there as soon as I can. What? What box? Yeah, uh huh." He yells real loud, "Elaine, did you get Thelma her personal items?"

"I told her I would and I did. She owes me five bucks. Why am I everybody's schlep n'fetch it?"

"What's for supper?" Uncle Sam takes the lid off the pot and inhales deeply.

Grandma gives him a taste off her big wooden spoon. "Your favorite! Veal paprikash."

"Well, hurry up and serve. I'm starving."

Grandma bangs the lid back on the pot. "We wait for *Apoukah*! He's the *mishgeeach* today butchering extra meat at the packing plant. And he has to be the *shoichet* in the chicken store. A lot of customers lately for the holidays. Trouble is, they only paid him with a chicken last week. We need the money more. But the chicken at least will be a good *Shabbes* dinner after I fatten it up; it will be just right. Tonight, we eat paprikash. And—we wait!"

Uncle Sam slurps a big piece of veal out of the pot.

"*Nein, nein!*" Grandma always yells no at everyone for trying to eat out of the pot. Uncle Sam just laughs at her.

Daddy is nodding and uh-huhing into the phone. "Yeah, yeah, I'm coming. I told you that already." He angrily hangs up the receiver and runs out the screen door waiting a few minutes to catch his breath.

I stop the rocking chair, holding on and almost standing up. "Daddy, what about my teacher meeting on Thursday? The teacher wants to talk to you 'bout my…"

"Let your Aunt Elaine take you. I've got an appointment with a customer."

Grandma comes to the door and shouts at Daddy's back. "Avraham, *vie gehst du?* It is supper. Aach!" She is disgusted and waves the spoon at his back. Daddy walks off the porch and starts across the street. He doesn't have his coat or hat on. I rock furiously back and forth, back and forth.

Eva comes out and shakes the bathroom rugs with a snap off the porch. She grabs a broom and sweeps. Then she just sits down on the steps and pulls a cigarette pack out of her apron pocket and lights one up. She holds her head with both hands and lets a big stream of smoke out onto the porch. I begin fanning the smoke away from my face.

"Why do you smoke? It makes me cough!"

"Vhy dey yell? It make me deaf! Dey ist cookoo, duh whole bunch. It crazy here. I no clean dis house nudder minute." Eva is always threatening to quit. She gets up and bangs the screen door behind her. I hear her hollering at Grandma. Then she comes back out—coat half on, a babushka tied under her chin and a shopping bag on her arm. Grandma's right behind waving her arms.

"Eva, Eva, *vait*, please! You know I count on you." She sounds like Eva.

"I go, missus. No work for dis crazy fam'ly no more. You no pay enuf for such yellin' en' screamin' en' dirty words."

Grandma takes a dollar bill out of the change purse tucked inside her undershirt and presses the bill into Eva's hand. "I was planning to raise you this month anyways. We start today, OK?"

Eva takes the bill and puts it into her bosom, nodding reluctantly as she turns back into the house. Grandma follows talking about leftover paprikash she will have for Eva's family.

I just rock.

Chapter Eight

CHOLENT AND CHICKEN FEATHERS
APRIL 1943

When Aunt Elaine goes to school for the teacher meeting, she finds out I'm not doin' so good on the tests. The truth is my 'rithmetic and English has got pretty bad. When I don't get into the special class called gifted, I'm ready to cry. First I think the class is about presents like a birthday or something. But Aunt Elaine explains it to me and Grandma that changing schools put me behind a little and I would have to study extra hard just to catch up. "The gifted is for kids way ahead."

When gifted people get French and other things I don't know nothin' about, I have to stay with Miss Steiner. She makes me do my times tables over and over. I'm not allowed to use my fingers for counting up. And I have a lotta extra homework to bring home. My book bag's getting awful heavy. Grandma tries to get me to take some things out of my bag.

"Why do you have to schlep everything, Sorahlah? Your back's already round."

I need to have my pomes and my piano books close to me ready just in case Miss Allison from Crescent School shows up at Colfax. The whole fall and winter goes flyin' by and no Miss Allison. I figger what with all the gifted stuff, there's no time for music lessons. I sneak into Mrs. Wolf's house—the other half of our double—and practice on her big baby grand piano when I should be doing the extra homework. Then I work till midnight at the kitchen table on my school stuff.

But no matter how hard I try, not bein' in the gifted class and dressin' like the other kids doesn't get me friends. Every day I put up with the girls who point at my buckle shoes and boys who pull my pigtails and knock my glasses off when we're in line. Hardest thing's trying to talk like the other kids in the class. They talk different than me. Kinda' like Eva talks different than Grandma and Grandpa. I have a real hard time changing from school talk to Yiddish or Hunky talk or Eva talk. It makes me remember how Miss Allison told me I need to learn to speak correctly for the recital. I try watching and saying things more like I'm suppost tuh do. "Pihahno," I repeat over and over to myself. "Say it right!" I listen real hard and ask Miss Campbell, the nice library lady, to help me. She gives me some good storybooks to read. She calls 'em plays.

"Listen to the dialogue in your head, Shirley. You'll learn lots from reading."

But they're hard and I don't get all the words right.

Gym class is the worst! When the girls see me take my clothes off to put on my gym suit, they laugh at my baby undershirt and cotton pants. I try to get Grandma to understand.

"Sorahlah, stop struggling. It is shameful for a girl not to have on a *hemdi* under her dress."

"Undershirt, Grandma, undershirt. Speak English. Today is gym, and all the other girls will laugh at me. They already do with my ugly glasses. Besides, I've got a slip on."

"A *hemdi*—ach—an undershirt's a good thing in the cold winter."

"It's almost spring, Grandma. Ouch, you're making my braids too tight."

Grandma pulls my slip on over my undershirt and is busy brushing and plaiting my hair. "Stand still, I need to get this gum band on your hair."

"Ouch! Ooh! That hurts, Grandma. I hate these pigtails."

"Don't use that *trayfe* word!" She gives my hair an extra pull when I use the p-i-g word.

"I jus' said the word p-i-g. I didn't eat any."

"Shah!" Grandma spits on her hands and smoothes my hair down on top.

"Good morning, missus." Eva comes through the back door removing her babushka.

"You are late!" Grandma is not pleased.

"The streetcar, missus, it break down. The pole fall off dat vire vhat shoots sparks, yuh know."

"Hurry and change; I have a lot of work today."

"You got lotta voik alla time." Eva trundles down to the basement.

"And no smoking in the basement. Go out in the backyard to smoke."

Grandma finishes her daily inspection of me by taking my face in her hands, brushing off some invisible crumbs with her dishtowel, and planting a solid kiss on my forehead.

"Oy, yoy, my *shaynical*, my *maidlach*. Now take your bag and don't forget your lunch. And put your glasses back on." Grandma mostly talks to the family in Hungarian and to me in mish mash Yiddish. But I'm happy with the way she takes care of me and watches out for my little sister even though I complain a lot.

I open my lunch bag and sniff. "It's bologna! Goody, I can't stand the salami. It smells up the whole cloakroom. Did you remember the pickles and mustard? Mmmm, an apple. I need a nickel for milk." I put on my clunky glasses.

"For *shamet zee*, no milk with meat. Drink water from the fountain."

I check my school bag. "My book of pomes—where is it? Oh, there it is. I've just written a new pome, Grandma."

Somehow writing words and rhyming is the one thing I do real good and better than the kids in the gifted class. I get to be the best speller and look up words in the dictionary on the homeroom windowsill. When there's a spelling bee, I get picked first by the leader. It's the only time I get picked!

"What's your new pome, Sorahlah?"

"'The Amazon.' I'm writing a pome about the Amazon. It's so dark and mysterious. We're readin'—oops, I mean *reading about* it in jography."

"The Amazon? Jography? What! *Ich weist nicht.*"

"English, Grandma, please. How will you pass your citizenship test if you don't talk American? Just say I don'—do not know." I have taken to correcting Grandma while I'm correcting myself. Grandma's looking through my book. I know she can't read it.

"Is this the book your mama gave you?"

"Uh, huh. Grandma, where's my blue music book?" I'm frantic.

"I put it away. There's no money for lessons. You shouldn't of asked Mrs. Wolf to use her piano. I don't vant charity from next door!"

"*Want*, Grandma, not *vant*. My book…where's my blue book?"

"In the dining room—in de—uh—the sideboard. Why do you schlep that book anyway?"

"I hope Miss Allison's coming to our school soon. Maybe she'll let me watch the lessons. Maybe she'll put me into the blue level book again when she sees I can play the whole red book better than before mother di—we had to move."

"How could you play it? You have no place to practice."

"Oh, I practice next, uh, to my classroom. There's a piano, uh, in the gym." Grandma almost catches me telling a lie.

"What are you talking about? You are not going next door to Mrs. Wolf, are you? Stay away from our landlady. Your grandfather will take a fit."

Eva comes back up the stairs with an apron on and a scarf around her head. "Ahkai, missus, vere I start?"

Grandma suddenly forgets about the piano next door and turns her attention to Eva. "Same as last week. It's Monday, isn't it? Upstairs, the beds first. Take the bucket and broom. And bring down the feather quilts to air outside."

"But, Missus, it too cold for hanging out…"

"If you smoke out there, you can hang out there. And spring is already here!" Grandma has an answer for all arguments. "Sorahlah, put on your coat—the one Aunt Elaine brought home. It's still too cold to go without one. Ach, the phone! Come straight home from school, Sor." And she runs to pick up the phone.

"Ahiee gotta do for no good money such teengs." Eva gathers the bucket and rags and puts the carpet sweeper under her arm.

"Why are you a maid, Eva?" I am curious about Eva.

"My fam'ly ain't no rich like yuns."

"I bet you could get a job like my Aunt Elaine in the Frank & Seder store. You could get lots of stuff cheap for your family, too."

"Youse OK, kid." She pats me on my head.

Grandma puts her hand over the receiver and speaks to Eva. "The bathroom rugs need a good shaking, too." Eva just shrugs her shoulders.

"Sorahlah, no food from the other children. They're *trayfe!*" Grandma keeps trying to convince me that kosher eating and drinking is what the good Lord expects. Everything else is *trayfe*, not kosher.

May

"Grandma, Grandma! Guess what? She came; she came." I'm so excited and out of breath, I can hardly speak.

"*Shaah shtill!* How many times did I tell you not to bang the screen door? Your grandfather is *dahven*ing." Grandma is moving her lips along with Grandpa.

"Ohhhhahhhmayne!" Grandpa sings the Amen at the top of his lungs.

"But, Grandma, she came. Miss Allison came and she says…" I'm beside myself.

"No! You know what I said about the money!" Grandma starts to busy herself peeling onions.

"But she says I don't have to pay."

"Hah! Nothing is for nothing. Now stop insisting!"

"But, she understands we don', I mean, do not have the money."

"Don't tell strangers your personal business."

"But, Grandma, she…"

"Quiet, your grandfather is practicing."

I can see that talk about piano lessons at school is over. Grandma starts peeling onions. She hands me the garbage from the onion peels and I wrap them in a newspaper and put them in the can under the sink. I peek around the kitchen door at Grandpa, who is singing the Hebrew like he's in a race with himself.

"Why does Grandpa have to practice so much?"

"He is leading the *Havdahlah* service on Saturday at the *shul*. Don't forget, he expects you to go with him, Sorahlah."

"But he's done it a hundred times already. Doesn't he know it yet?"

"He practices so that he will be perfect. Now wash your hands and sit down and have a cookie with some milk." Then Grandma hollers down to the basement, "Eva, don't forget to take the bread and the fish for your mother."

Eva yells back as she comes up with her coat on. "Tanks, missus. My fam'ly like how you cook. Sorah, I jus clean floor! No crumbs, kid!"

"Please come early tomorrow. I have to cook the chicken first." Grandma is wrapping the leftovers for Eva.

I make a face in disgust. "Not that poor little chicken still running around in the basement?"

"Tonight you will see how I get it ready and help me pull the feathers off."

"Not me, never...never. Oh, Grandma! It's just a little chicken."

"You see how she put a bag over chicken head 'n..." Eva draws her finger across her neck and makes a noise with her throat to show somebody's throat getting cut like in the movies.

I react quickly. "How can you? The poor chicken doesn't have a chance. It's...it's primitive like in the Amazon! Eva, you can help Grandma with the chicken! You can do it same as you do for your grandma."

"I ain't got no grandma 'n I no get paid for poorin' blood outta' chicken neck! No here! No home! Eet primitive! 'Sides, I gotta do 'nuf odder teengs vid vorshin' 'n aironin' 'n scrubbin' 'n takin' everybody trash outta here. I no got time for no more voik. I go, missus. See you Friday, maybe." With that Eva laughs and bangs the screen door on her way out.

"What! What? You know I'm counting on you, Eva! It's *Shabbes* tomorrow," Grandma shouts at Eva's back.

I yell at Grandma in disgust. "It's not right to kill that poor chickie even if you do put his head in a bag!"

"You like to eat the soup, Sorahlah? You need to pluck feathers."

I'm good at changing the subject. "Grandma, can I have another cookie? Please?"

Grandma takes the cookie out of a jar she keeps on the bottom shelf of the cupboard. "Sorahlah, now don't you bother your grandfather, and don't copy him! Give the pot a stir and if it boils too fast, turn the gas down."

"But how do I know if it's too fast?" I can hear the pot start to bubble and I smell the food real strong. I'm afraid to pull a chair over to the stove. *Uh, uh! No way. I did that once and it was almost a real disaster with the pot and with me!* I flip the knob on the stove to off.

I hear Grandpa coughing as he is trying to sing. I sneak up behind him as he clears his throat and takes a small pill from a little box in his pocket and puts it in his mouth. His mouth chews while he is mumbling the prayers. I smell licorice just like the black chewy candy my bubbie used to have in her candy store. When I tried it, it made my tongue and teeth all black. I wonder if his mouth is black. I try wiggling to see his face just as he begins with the knee bends, his head jiggling from side to side. My mistake is I also start singing right along with him without meaning to.

Grandpa turns angrily on me, shouting to Grandma, *"Onyoukah, Onyoukah,* Malvina, she's doing it again!" He throws his hands up in frustration, sending his yarmulke flying.

"What, *Apoukah?* What? No one is killing you. What is she doing?"

"She is trying to sing with me. She is making fun on me. She is not allowed. It is not allowed. No women! No women! Only men sing the service. Take her out of here."

"Sorahlah, no more singing, you hear? *Genick!"* Grandma has hold of my arm.

"But, Grandma, I was just trying to see if Grandpa's mouth was black from the licorice candy…"

"Voos? What? Candy? Black licorice? *Shah, shtill!* Into the kitchen." With that Grandma puts an apron around me and sets me at the table peeling a bag of potatoes. "I told you not to copy. It is not proper for a girl. Ach! The gas went out under the pot."

"But, Grandma, I want to sing like Grandpa."

"Shah, it is not allowed in the *shul*—or in the dining room." She knew what I was about to say.

"Why can't I be a cantor in the synagogue, too, like Grandpa?"

"You can sing but not with the men. It is never allowed!" She takes the potatoes out of my hands. I really make a crooked job of peeling them; Grandma is trying to save the potatoes from the garbage.

"Why isn't it allowed? I don't understand." Through a crack in the door I watch Grandpa fold his *tallis*. He takes the black straps off his arm and the little black box off his forehead (I think he calls them factories or something like that) and folds everything neatly into a black velvet bag.

"You must know your place, Sorahlah!" Grandpa shouts in an angry voice as he comes into the kitchen. "It is about time you knew that men are in charge of the *shul* and praying." Then Grandpa inhales deeply and clucks his tongue. "*Onyoukah*, what is in the pot?"

"*Cholent* for Saturday lunch, *Apoukah*. But no tasting; it's not finished cooking."

"*Oy, Onyoukah.*" Grandpa continues inhaling the steam rising out of the pot.

I say, "Why do you both use that Hunky language? Call her Mother and he's Father. You will never sound like Americans."

Grandpa yelling at me puts me in a real talk back mood! He glares at me. "Show some respect for the language of the family."

"I'm an American not a Hunky and I hate that pot of bean stuff— in Hungarian or English. And call me Shirley! It's more American." Feeling really brave, I add, "And I will take those lessons from Miss Allison for free, and I will sing in the synagogue."

Grandpa is horrified. "We do not accept charity. And if you try to sing, I will not take you to *shul* Saturday. Do not shame me! Do you hear?"

That is not a punishment I want. I look forward to Saturday night at the Poale Zedek Synagogue and hearing Grandpa sing— and grabbing a piece of herring. So I nod but cross my fingers behind my back.

Chapter Nine

THE PEDDLER MAN
JUNE 1943

Early June is dry, and leaves and grass are crackling for water. The zinnias and cosmos still bloom but need daily drinks from the hose. I like this job. It gives me a chance to play with a stray cat that followed me home several days ago. I pour little dabs of milk in a jar lid I hide under the bushes where Grandma can't see the cat.

"Do not feed that *ketzele*! Do you hear me, Sorahlah? We have enough trouble feeding ourselves let alone all the strays off the street." So far Grandma has not caught me.

"Knives sharpened! Any umbrellas? Broken umbrellas fixed. Knives sharpened for *Shabbes*! Kitchen towels! New colored kitchen towels. Housedresses! Knives sharpened. Sweet meats! Sweet meats for good children. Sweet meats! Knives, scissors sharpened…" The peddler man half hanging off his wagon sings his list of goods and goodies. His horse clops right along with the song!

Full of excitement, I drop the hose—watering the cat, the porch, and the screen door.

"Mr. Peddler man, Mr. Peddler man. Do you have any sweet meats for me? Do you have my new socks? Grandma promised me some regular new socks like the other girls wear. Grandma, he's here." I sing my own answer just like him. "The peddler man is here. Come quick! He's bringing lots of good things and pretty ones, too. Do you have the new tablecloth for *Shabbes*? Grandma! C'mon, 'fore he doesn't have anymore."

The peddler man pulls up his wagon close to the curb. The horse stops, nods his head, and nibbles grass sticking out of the red brick street. I start backing up to the porch as far away from the horse as possible—the smell—the snorting—the large ugly foot that smacks the street. The peddler lets the reins down over the horse's head and goes around to the back of his wagon. He reaches into packages wrapped in brown paper, coming up with a pair of white and navy socks.

"And your socks!" He holds them high and I want to get them out of his hand, but I'm afraid of the horse. "My horse won't hurt you. Gentle as a lamb, especially with little girls."

I bravely come to the curb. "And my socks, Grandma! He has the socks you ordered for me."

Grandma appears at the screen door. "I'm coming! I'm coming. Ach! Why is the floor so wet?" Grandma doesn't mind the horse at all and offers him an apple out of her apron pocket. I make a face as the horse shows his ugly teeth gobbling the apple. "So, Yankel, what do you have today? Let me see the tablecloths. My son spilled wine on my one good cloth last Friday night. Not even Eva could get out that stain! It's ruined."

"It's easier to get the *shmutz* out of the shirt collars in this town, that's for sure." He unpacks his wares from the back of the truck along with a grinding wheel and some umbrellas.

"Here, Sorahlah, some sweet meats special for you. No charge!"

"Mmmmm, thank you." I keep one eye on the horse—slobbering, nodding, and pawing.

"Here, missus, special for you, a beautiful brand new tablecloth with flowers around the edge and napkins to match. A real bargain." The peddler opens the cloth and gives it a good snap to show how beautiful it is.

"No, no! White! Only white for the Sabbath."

"But it is just like the one I sold Mrs. Wolf over on Melvin Street."

"She's not married to my husband! White! Only white will do."

I already have my new socks on. "Look, Grandma, perfect fit. Is that Milton Wolf's mother, Mr. Peddler man?"

The peddler nods and hands Grandma a white tablecloth and a flowered apron.

"Oh, I know Miltie Wolf. He walks me home from Hebrew school."

Grandma is pulling the apron over her head. "What? A boy! Sorahlah, no boys! You are too young!"

"Oh, Grandma. He teaches the younger children about the holidays. He wants to be a—? What's that word that means helper—uh, assistant. He wants to be the *rebbe's* assistant."

The peddler laughs. "A rabbi's assistant! Nah! Not little Miltie?"

"Oh, yes. He's not little anymore. He's studying for his Bar Mitzvah already."

Grandma reaches into her dress and pulls out her change purse.

The peddler is quick to add to the sale. "How about a new housedress, missus?"

"Just give me the socks, the white tablecloth, and this apron."

"Something else, please. I won't be back till next spring."

"Fer voos nicht?"

"Yes, why not? I chime in. Where are you going?" I am looking quickly through the other socks.

"Your husband, Rabbi Fischel, hired me to be his assistant—in the slaughterhouse. I'm going to help make sure everything is kosher!"

"Ugh! That's a terrible job!" I don't like it when Grandpa takes me along and makes me watch how he cuts the poor little cow's throat. I have to sit on the wooden edge of the platform, swinging my legs and hiding my eyes till it's over.

Grandma replies sharply, "Someone has to do it! Two dishtowels then—pretty ones with pictures—not the flour sacks this time." The peddler takes his pencil and wets it with his tongue and writes down the total.

"And another pair of socks, in pink, please," I add.

Grandma nods in agreement and counts out the money.

Then Grandma takes her scissors out of her housedress pocket. "And my scissors need sharpened! Here's the extra nickel. Come in when you're done. I made cheese pockets and also some with *lekvar*! The water is boiling for tea."

The peddler puts the money carefully in a little box under the brown packages. He starts pumping with his foot and grinding the blades. The horse shakes his head at the noise.

"I can see why you do this job! You get everybody's fresh cakes." I take the pink socks out of the package.

"Not everyone feeds me like your grandma. She is very generous with me and my horse. And her Hungarian cheese pockets are the best."

"I like the other kind! The prune." I skip happily into the kitchen licking my lips in anticipation. "I'll take one, too, Grandma, please."

"Not until you wash your hands. You have been watering and playing with that cat. With *lekvar* or cheese?"

I cannot look Grandma in the eye. "The prune ones—uh, *lekvar*—please."

The peddler man comes in with the scissors. He washes his hands and takes a seat at the table. "And if you don't mind, two sugar cubes to make the tea sweet when I swallow, missus."

"With my baking, you don't need to hold sugar between your teeth. You should be working for me! I need an assistant in plucking feathers." Grandma takes a brown paper bag and heads down the cellar steps. "When you are done with your tea, Sorahlah, downstairs!"

The peddler man glances over his shoulder, takes two sugar cubes, and fixes them between his front teeth. One tooth is bright gold. Then he pours the tea into the saucer and begins slurping and swallowing loudly. He bites into the cheesecake, parking the sugar in his cheek. "Ah, a *mechaiyah*—really delicious."

The chicken screams wildly from downstairs. I cover my ears. The sudden squawk tells me that the deed is done! Grandma calls loudly and insistently, "Sorahlah! Come down here, young lady. It's time for you to help pluck the feathers. Sooraahlaah...!"

"Mr. Peddler man, do you still have those saddle shoes from the last time you were here? I 'd like to try them on." I follow him out the screen door making sure it doesn't bang.

Chapter Ten

KENNYWOOD PARK
JULY 1943

As it turns out, I do not make it to hear Grandpa sing that Friday in June. It starts with a cough and a runny nose and then funny lookin' splotches on my tummy and I am "confined to my room" as Dr. Saul puts it. He climbs those steps two at a time when Grandma calls him half yelling. He takes my temperchur and examines my stomach and then says she's garanteed or something like that. Aunt Elaine says, "It's the chicken pox, which means no school or visitors or playing outside. And above all, no scratching." And, yow, I itch every which way. My little sister gets it, too, but not so bad as me. We're covered in pink lotion and get our meals on a tray. Grandma is up and down the steps every time me or my sister want some attention. Seems like a thousand times a day! Finally when I call her just to straighten my covers on the bed, Grandma loses patience. "*Genick*! No more up and down." She has me ring a little bell and I yell down and she yells back upstairs.

Aunt Elaine brings me my homework from school and plugs a radio in next to my bed so I can listen to stuff when I eat lunch. "The Shadow" is my favorite and "I Love a Mystery" is next. I even get to listen to "Stella Dallas" and "Our Gal, Sunday." It sure seems dumb to me having a day of the week for a name! Best of all is reading lots of books and the plays Miss Campbell, the librarian, lets my aunt check out. My reading gets real good after I go through *Heidi, Jane Eyre, Little Women,* and *Dr. Doolittle.* But the plays she sends are still too hard to follow. The lines people speak keep jumping around.

What's not so good is I don't have the piano lessons. But Miss Allison writes me a nice letter about how I could take in the fall when school starts again. I miss all the final tests, but they still let me pass to Grade 4. School is over, and at least I don't have to worry about taking off my gym suit in front of the other girls. The white and brown saddle shoes are still in my prayers at bedtime. Then Grandma makes a big promise. Since I am so sick, she will ask the peddler man to give Grandpa the saddle shoes for some extra assistant salary. Grandpa just gives in since I'm sick. And come July, I am gonna be allowed to go to the Squirrel Hill Kennywood picnic. Pretty soon I am no longer itching and Aunt Elaine is glad that my face doesn't have pockmarks. But Grandma still does not grab and kiss her *shayna punim.*

One good thing is that Daddy and Uncle Sam keep away from me. Something about men getting the pox means they can't get fertilized. I don't understand what that has to do with a garden and growing flowers or vegetables unless they couldn't pee no more. I know my cousin Sammy thinks it's real funny when he pees in the yard and says he's fertilizing the grass. Grandma tells me to "*shah shtill,* nice girls don't talk like that." At least, nobody can poke fun at me or grab my braids.

It's great having lots of quiet time to myself with no yelling 'bout my posture or grades in school. I 'specially like reading and reading and reading. I ask my aunt to get me some more adventure books 'bout *Sherlock Homes* and the *Bobby Twins.*

And then I discover *Gone with the Wind* stuffed in the bottom of my aunt's cupboard. Aunt Elaine says it's too racy a novel for young girls when she catches me with it and puts it back on the top shelf where she thinks I can't reach it. But I drag the bench from Grandma's dressing table and climb up stretching on my toes. The book practically hits my head and I fall off the bench. It sounds like a clap of thunder when it hits the floor.

"Vat's da noise, Sorahlah?" Eva yells up from the living room where she is sweeping, redding up, and dusting.

"Nothing, uh, Eva. I just tripped on a chair," I holler back down. But reading that book is worth everything even though I have to sneak at night with a flashlight under my covers. I can pretend I'm

Scarlet madly in love with Mr. Butler. *Whew! I don't know if I'll ever finish that story. So many pages!*

Everything stays that way until Kennywood Day arrives. Grandma and Aunt Elaine spend a whole night getting the picnic supper together. The house smells of fried chicken and boiling potatoes with hard cooked eggs. They wash and pack grapes in old flour sack towels along with purple plums and juicy peaches. Grandma peels and slices a huge black radish. She spreads it with chicken schmaltz, which Grandpa says is a *maichel,* delicious. He always licks his lips, but the chicken fat really makes his beard greasy and stinky. I try a bite just once and it puts my mouth on fire. The ice-man brings a big block of ice and breaks it into pieces so it fits in the basket to keep the food from spoiling. There are ice trays Grandma has been saving in the top part of the icebox for weeks ready to dump in the fresh tea and lemonade. But the best of all is a huge jar of kosher sour pickles from the crocks in the base-ment. My mouth gets all wrinkled just thinking about those pick-les. By the time the potato salad is ready to be mixed, Grandma has folded an old bed sheet up over the basket to use as a tablecloth and has two weeks worth of Yiddish newspapers ready to spread on the wooden table and picnic benches.

The best things I love are the little nut cookies and a delicious seven layer cake with whipped up chocolate icing. "Dobos Torte," Uncle Sam calls it, "like they make in the Old Country." Then just in case the men are still hungry, Grandpa lays a round watermelon on the floor of the car right under my sister's feet. It's her job to use her feet to keep it from rolling around.

We have to park what seems like a hundred miles from the picnic tables. Everyone has to carry something. I take the bag of the oldest silverware and a bunch of different colored cups. Daddy says they are something real new out of 'luminum. It's hard to carry, but I would not let anyone hear me huff or puff or wipe away one bit of 'spiration offa my nose. I just lick the drips—salt and all—and keep my mouth shut. Daddy carries the basket and ice on his shoulder, and my uncle has the watermelon under his arm and the jug of tea swinging from his other arm. Grandpa and

Grandma sit with the basket at a table under a tree in a shady part of the picnic place.

Aunt Elaine grabs my little sister and they go off to Kiddie Land. I can't be in Kiddie Land 'cause I'm taller than the cutout of Skippy. So my father and Uncle Sam pull my arm between them and drag me off to the rides. Aunt Elaine has tickets she bought at school before it let out for the summer so we don't have to stand in line except for the rides. Daddy and Uncle Sam hold onto my arms for The Old Mill.

I remember the last time I went to the Kennywood picnic. My mommy took me even with her big belly to the merry-go-round and on the kiddie rides. I was never real good at anything that twirls too fast, so she let me pick out what I wanted to ride. The train was my favorite and I liked to throw a line in water to play fish or throw balls up a circle that could get you a prize if you got the right number of points. Daddy said it was a waste of good ride tickets.

That last time, we went with Grandma and Grandpa and met Bubbie and Aunt Mayme there. My cousins Marilyn and Sammy got on the same rides as me, but I was more scared of the dark and didn't want to go into The Old Mill. The boat smelled and the dark in the tunnel made me shiver. People would make real scary noises and scream so loud you could hear it echoing over and over. Noah's Ark was the same way with scary things jumpin' out at you and the boat rocking and rocking. I always had to hide my face in Mommy's arm till Mommy said, "Here's the exit, Sor." Sammy wanted to go on the pony rides so Mommy let the man put me up on top of a horse, too. It started to walk and follow the other horse with Sammy. I kept slipping from side to side. I knew I was gonna' fall off. Mommy jus' waved at me when I came 'round the circle and the man took me off before my turn was done. It sure wasn't like it looked in the cowboy movies. My mother said I never had to go on those rides again.

But here we are, Daddy and my uncle with me between in line for The Old Mill. I start to say I won't get in the boat. Then Uncle Sam tells me to quit whining like a baby, and Daddy says he will give me something to whine about. I don't dare refuse to get in the boat after that. They are laughing and making fun of the boys and girls who are already hugging each other. I don't know what's so funny. The smell's the same. There are some flashing lights and spooky ghosts that keep popping out, but I just close my eyes until it's all over.

Then Uncle Sam buys some fuzzy pink stuff called cotton candy and I try it. It makes my face and fingers sticky, and my stomach makes strange noises. Before I can say no, we are in line for the roller coaster. I start to plead with my father. "No, no, Daddy, it's too fast." I'm really afraid of going up high. *My one other trip to a fair in the neighborhood put me up on a Ferris wheel next to my cousin Sammy, who rocked the chair at the top lookin' over the whole world. It was terrible and I almost wet my pants.* Now here I am ready to go even higher and faster. I start to pull away from my father, but he grabs my arm and forces me into a seat. I do not want to cry; all the other people in the seats are screaming and laughing. My neck feels hot and my mouth turns dry.

"What's wrong with you?" Daddy's voice is right at my ear and he is yelling.

"Do you want people to think you're a sissy?"

And the coaster starts climbing, up, up, up! Until suddenly it drops and my stomach drops with it. My bottom flies up as the car goes down throwing my body hard against my father, who has his arm around me.

"See, nothing to be 'fraid of! Let go of the bar and put your hands up like everybody else."

Instead I close my eyes and hold on even tighter. I feel the sweetness of the pink cotton candy coming back up my throat and when the coaster drops again and curves around, I gag horribly, sending all kinds of vomit onto the new shirt Grandma bought for me.

"Oh, fer crissakes, Shirley, look what you've done now." Vomit is on Daddy's white pants! And all over his brown and white shoes! He is not laughing or screaming at that moment.

When we get off the ride, Uncle Sam thinks it's really a big joke. Daddy points me in the direction of the picnic tables and tells me to get Grandma to clean me up. I see the two of them enter a building marked restrooms. I can hardly see my way to the picnic table, but I remember there's a lake with rowboats on the way. I cross a bridge over the lake. Then there's Grandma setting the table and getting the food out.

"Oy, Sorahlah, what happened?" She pours some of the melted ice water onto a hanky and cleans off my face and then my shirt. She rattles off furiously to Grandpa about letting a child walk in the park alone and lets me sip cold water from one of the cups.

"She needs to get stronger and grow up." Grandpa is already sampling a piece of chicken. My stomach is not in the mood for the lunch, not even the pickles or the cookies that everyone's eating. Aunt Elaine gets angry when Uncle Sam tells her what a big scaredy cat I am. Daddy just fills a plate full of food and moves away from me.

"Shirley Ruth, you shtink from vomit." He holds his nose. "Sit over on the grass."

I can smell myself, sour and sweaty.

I never want to go to Kennywood again.

Chapter Eleven

MY GRANDMA'S SHABBES GOY
SEPTEMBER 1943

I sit on the closed toilet seat in the bathroom and neatly tear off squares of toilet paper and put them in several piles along a small table with a towel rack attached. My friend Gracie Pasternak who lives around the corner on Pittock Street leans against the bathtub and watches with great curiosity.

I count, "One, two, three four—? Aunt Elaine, Uncle Sam, Daddy, Grandpa, Grandma—uh, one, two, three, four, five. Wait a minute, I must have forgot somebody."

Grandma calls up loudly. "Sorahlah? Are you tearing the toilet paper? Don't forget six piles and don't drop any on the floor."

"But I keep counting and get only five piles. I forgot somebody!"

Gracie lights up. "Sorahlah, yourself! You did not count yourself."

"I am...I'm such a dummy."

"Stop that, Sor. You are not a dummy." Gracie's my one true friend.

Why I always forget to remember myself is a mystery. We laugh as toilet paper begins to flutter to the floor. "Let's see, where was I? I need to catch up on my own pile of toilet paper." I try to hurry and end up with more on the floor and in the wastebasket. "This is such a waste of time when I could be practicing the piano next door."

Gracie whispers, "Next door? But your grandma says..."

"Yes, yes. I know Grandma says we don't have the money, but Miss Allison is giving me free lessons as long as I practice."

Gracie's helping me tear the paper. "But why next door?"

"They have a big piano—Mrs. Wolf calls it a baby grand—that sits in their living room. Not at all like the one at school. Mrs. Wolf told me I could come anytime as long as she is home. No one in her house plays it."

"Did you tell your grandparents about going next door?"

"No way! They'd really take a fit. A conniption fit!"

Gracie starts making a paper boat out of toilet paper. "Well, then, how?"

"I didn't tell anyone but you. You really know my darkest secrets, Gracie."

"Uh, oh! You're gonna get it from your father when he finds out."

"No one knows 'cept Mrs. Wolf, and she promises not to tell."

Grandma yells upstairs again. "Soraahlaaah!"

"I'm tearing, I'm tearing. One for Daddy, Auntie, Grandma, Grandpa, and of course me—and Uncle Sam," I yell back down the steps.

The phone rings and grandma hollers again.

"Sorahlah, the phone. Answer the phone! I have my hands in dough."

"But Grandma, it's not *Shabbes* yet. You told me never to answer the phone unless it's *Shabbes*."

"Just answer it and take the message. I'm waiting for a call from Mrs. Sobel about our Sunday pinochle game. Tell her I'll try to call her back before *Shabbes* begins."

I run down the steps and answer the phone. "Yes, oh hello, Mrs. Sobel. No, Grandma said I could answer this once. She will try to call you back before sundown. Me? I'm tearing the toilet paper." I nod and listen. "*Mishigus?* What's a *mishigus?* Is that like pinochle? Huh? Oh, OK. Yes, Mrs. Sobel. I'll ask her. You will bring the *mandelbrot.* Yes, I know what that is: the long hard cakes that Grandpa has to dip in his coffee when he takes out his teeth. Uh, huh. Thank you...yes...yes. I will give her the message. 'Bye. A good *Shabbes* to you, too."

I climb the stairs again. "Gracie, do you know what a *mishigus* is?" Gracie's lining up the toilet paper piles neatly.

"Well, my mother says it's doing things that really aren't in the Bible, but that somebody says is necessary according to the rabbi, like having to tear the toilet paper before *Shabbes* so you won't have to do any work on the Sabbath."

Gracie's parents are not very observant, as Grandma keeps telling me. But she likes Grace and lets her be my friend anyway.

I continue, "I guess tearing toilet paper is work?"

Gracie looks at the piles of paper. "Your family uses an awful lot of toilet paper."

Grandma hollers up again, "Did you get the message, Sor? Did you get it all correct?"

Gracie hollers back, "She got it! She got it!" Gracie continues, "Why aren't you supposed to answer the phone except on *Shabbes*?"

"Grandma says it's work. But Uncle Sam says I get all *his* messages wrong. Daddy told me I spoiled an important business call. But I know it was only his girlfriend, Thelma, that's who. And she doesn't like me much anyways. They're going to get married, you know, sometime soon."

Gracie gets excited. "Maybe you'll get to be a bridesmaid and wear a long dress."

"No chance. She's mad at me for peeking inside a box that got delivered here. I thought it was fancy wedding clothes for my sister and me. But she screamed and yelled that I had no business in her private things. It was really terrible. She cried and got what Uncle Sam says was hysterical over nothing, and my father made me apologize at least ten times. Then Thelma said that children couldn't come to her wedding—"no way" and I had a hard time swallowing food at the dinner table and my father kept telling me I better learn to do things correct 'cause she's gonna be my mother... and..." By this time my tears are falling on the toilet paper and I struggle to stay calm.

Gracie takes some paper off one of the piles and I blow my nose. She hugs me tight, and I can see the scar on her face she says came from a bad fall. I notice how yellow her eyes are and that she does not have pale skin like me. She straightens out the bathroom, folding the towels in place. Gracie tries to cheer me up and changes the subject. "Well, you took Mrs. Sobel's message just fine. Who cares about an old stepmother, anyway? And your grandma lets you do things for her that are important like tearing toilet paper and answering the phone on *Shabbes*."

"Oooh, and I turn the gas stove on and off to heat up the chicken soup and the *cholent* for Saturday and…" We both start to laugh.

"Wait a minute! I'm still confused. How come you're allowed and no one else is?"

"Grandma says she needs a *Shabbes goy* but can't afford one, and Eva won't work on the weekend so it's up to me."

"A *Shabbes* what?

"A *Shabbes goy*—a non Jew who works for the Jews on the Sabbath so they don't have to do it themselves."

"But you are Jewish…uh, aren't you?" Gracie is Jewish, too, but confused by all the things that go on in our family. "I guess you must be with a rabbi for a grandpa!"

I nod. "But Grandma says I'm young and will be forgiven by G."

"Who's G?"

"I'm not supposed to say that word."

"What word?"

"The G word!" I look around and loudly whisper, "God!"

Grandma suddenly appears at the top of the steps. "*Shamet zee!* Show some respect. Do not speak the good Lord's name." Gracie's mouth is hanging half open.

The phone rings again and I go to answer it. Grandma goes back down the steps. "No, it is not *Shabbes* yet. I'll get it this time. Hellooooo! No! I don't believe it! *Nem tudem.* Oy, yoy, yoy! And then Grandma listens, nodding in approval and clucking her tongue and rattling off in Hungarian.

Gracie rolls her eyes. "This is *mishigus* for sure, Sor!"

I shrug my shoulders and sigh. "So, I'm my grandmother's *Shabbes goy.*"

Gracie adds, "I guess I'm my family's *Shabbes goy* seven days a week! Do you at least get some allowance or something for doing this?"

"Oh, nothing. Grandpa says I should feel honored to do a *mitzvah* for the family on *Shabbes*."

Grandma concludes her conversation. "*A guten tag.* Yah, yah, good-bye. Sorahlah, finish with the tearing of the paper and take your bath. You will need to be clean for the *Havdalah* service tomorrow. Quick, before your grandpa wakes up and needs to use the bathroom. Go! Go!"

"I'm going, I'm going! Bye, Gracie. See you when we walk to school Monday. Oh, Grandma, I almost forgot, Mrs. Sobel is bringing the *mandelbrot*, the kind with almonds."

Grandma takes Gracie's hand and they go down the stairs. "Come, Grace, taste my chicken soup. Maybe it needs a little more *zaltz*."

Gracie, who loves Grandma's cooking, really works hard helping at home and is in charge of her brother and everything. I know she is hoping for more than just a taste. "You always make it just right. I hope you added extra carrots. Sor loves carrots."

I can't help but smile to myself. Gracie loves carrots even more than I do. I wait for Grandma's answer.

"There's plenty for your family, too!"

Good girl, Gracie—you know just what to say to Grandma! I splash into the tub and the spray wets the toilet paper and the floor. *Oy, oh, well—I'll make it dry.* I get out of the tub and wrap a big towel around myself. Then I blow on the wet paper hard and fan it with my towel. No good! It ends up on the floor and is more soaking wet. *Hmmm, Sorahlah, what to do now?* Then suddenly, I spot a matchbox high on the window ledge just poking out of the curtains. I hop on the toilet seat and climb up standing on my toes to reach. Down fall the matches along with a pack of Lucky Strike cigarettes right into the puddle on the floor. Quick, I rescue the cigarettes and the matches. *Hah! So that's how Uncle Sam sneaks up here to smoke on Shabbes.*

I gather the toilet paper into one neat pile and carefully strike a match on the box. This heat will dry it quick. But the match goes out. I strike a second one and wave the heat over the paper. It's working. Then somehow the curtains are in flames. I grab the glass from the sink and fill it with water throwing it over the flames. "*Oh, my God, my God! It's getting worse.* Grandma!" I begin to yell, but there she is already coming up the steps.

"What *geschmeks*? Such a *shtink*." She pushes me aside, pulling the curtains off the window, and grabs the towel, throwing it over the flaming paper and curtains and stomps it with both her feet. I am coughing from the smoke. Then she faces me. "Were you trying to smoke?"

"Me, smoke! Never, Grandma. I was just heating up the toilet paper," which is almost the truth.

"Go to your room, now! What a *mishuganah* business. Ach! Get dressed and downstairs immediately to set the table." Grandma opens the windows all over the second floor. The smoke is flowing out. She's cleaning the window, the floor, the tub, changing the towels, and putting a fresh roll of toilet paper out. I never saw the bathroom get so clean, not even by Eva.

I don't know what she tells the family, but somehow it all gets blamed on that hidden matchbox and something called spontaneous combustion. I know those words; we just learned safety stuff in science class. Uncle Sam doesn't say a word.

Grandpa sleeps through the whole thing. As for the *shtink*, Grandma tells him she burned the *cholent*! And nobody notices there's no torn toilet paper for *Shabbes*.

Chapter Twelve

MOVING EXPERIENCES
OCTOBER 1943 TO MAY 1944

On October 9, 1943, my father marries Thelma Friedman in the rabbi's study. The only thing my sister and I share from the wedding is a piece of cake and a family picture. Whatever is happening, I am the last to know. My father and Thelma move into a house on Pittock Street—just two doors away from my friend Gracie Pasternak. This is very exciting for me, except that Thelma doesn't care for "those refugees," as she refers to them. Thelma and Daddy are there by themselves until furniture for the house arrives, and Grandma can pack up my sister and me for the big move.

Daddy seems more pleased than he's been for a long time. The only thing is that he makes a big issue of my dealing with my stepmother, Thelma.

"You will call her Mother, do you hear me?"

"But she's not my mother. Why can't I just call her Thelma like you do?"

His face gets beet red and I can see his hand going for the fur whip he keeps behind the kitchen door. "You will do what I say—you and your sister. Now what are you gonna call her, Shirley?"

I am hesitant but know what I have to say to avoid a whipping.

"Mother." My voice is barely above a whisper.

"Louder, and give her a kiss."

"Mother!" I shout but stand rooted to the spot.

My sister runs and climbs into Thelma's lap and gives her a hug and gets hugged back. "Melma," Barbara laughs.

From this first moment, I know how it's going to be all the time. My little sister is petted and favored just like a small doll. I

am glad I can avoid that close contact, except I have to let my stepmother braid my hair and check my clothes and socks and stuff.
She is not happy about it.

"Stand still! I don't have all day to fuss over you. You're old enough
to braid your own hair." And she yanks my braid so hard, it makes me
yelp like a dog.

"Ooooooh—ouch—stop it—that hurts."

"Shut up, you spoiled brat. And look at your socks—not on
straight and your dress already has a stain. Your father expects me
to see that his girls look well kept. I'll get the blame for your slop-
piness. Get to school before you're late and the teacher calls home
again about your absences and lateness."

She shoves me out the door onto the porch and I don't have
my book bag and have to pound on the door again to get in, and
then my book of pomes and my music book are not in there and I
am shaking and about to cry. But I don't wanna be late again. "I'll
look for my stuff when I get home after school," I mutter to myself.
Gracie is way ahead of me, and so I gallop like some kind of horse
to make it before the late bell rings.

After living on Pittock Street for four months, I get in the habit
of stopping at Grandma's to get a cookie and some milk. I really
miss my grandma and the life there. Grandma keeps asking me if
everything is all right. I just smile and tell her that Barbara is real
happy and I am getting along fine. She looks at me and says nothing. I have scratches on my face from Thelma using the comb too
close to my cheeks when she pulls the knots out. Then she notices
that there is a bunch of blood on the top of my head.

"Why is your head bloody, Sorahlah?" She takes a washrag and
wipes my head with warm water from the tea kettle.

"Ow, my head is sore, Grandma."

"*Fer voos?* What is making it bleed so? Are you picking at a scab
or what?"

"I got chewing gum in my hair and when I tried to get it out my
hair came out, too."

"Cows chew, not people!" Grandma is not a fan of chewing
gum.

But I know better than to tell her that my stepmother pulled my hair out this morning when she tried to get the rubber bands loose after I did my own plaits and made a mess of it. Thelma just grabbed and pulled, and I cried so hard I couldn't stop and she screamed even louder.

"Shut up! I'll give you something to cry about." And she slapped my face so hard I almost fell over. It was all I could do to grab my book bag, put on a coat, and get out of her way.

That day in school, I just don't say anything even when I know the answers to the teacher's questions. I just sit and cover my face with my hands. I don't even talk to Gracie or anybody. I don't eat anything 'cause I forgot my lunch bag and milk money and just take a drink from the fountain and spend a lotta time in the bathroom. By the afternoon, the teacher brings me my brown lunch bag.

"Your mother says you forgot this and also sends a nickel for your milk. Sit down, Shirley, and eat and I'll get you some milk. You should have told me you forgot your lunch. You need to learn to be more responsible." She looks at me funny, and when she walks away, I throw the lunch, which is always cheese, in the garbage can in the girl's bathroom. I just leave the milk on the windowsill and try to take a deep breath and think why my stepmother brought me the lunch. Maybe she's sorry she made me cry. But my day is still horrible and my face is chapped and my stomach hurts and as soon as the bell rings, I go to Grandma's as fast as I can, and after she questions me about my hair, I run home.

Usually when I get home, I do chores like set the table and make my bed and my sister's bed and pick up the newspapers and put them in a pile by the side door to the basement. I try to make up for my bad day and make my father's bed, too. Thelma is never home. She parks Barbara with my grandma and is off doing something for my uncle's fur business. My father is working for my uncle Sam in his fur store right on the corner of Beacon and Murray Avenue. He wants to learn the fur trade so he can earn what he says is "real money." But Daddy does not like working for his brother and complains that he hardly gets a decent day's wages.

"They fight," my stepmother tells Aunt Elaine, "like cats and dogs."

Thelma tries real hard to satisfy my father by learning how to cook all his favorite foods. Even Grandma, who gives her the recipes, says, "Thelma's a real cook and baker." I never complain about the endless cheese sandwiches for lunch 'cause supper's always good. But my father's so angry with his brother for not paying him enough that Thelma says, "He just chews and swallows but doesn't enjoy all her hard work in the kitchen." I love the steak or veal paprikash and especially the big bowls of vegetable soup, my favorite. The one thing that makes Thelma smile is when I ask for another serving of her soup or roast.

At night Thelma and my father are the ones fighting like cats and dogs. It keeps getting worse and worse. My father starts with the throwing and breaking of dishes. I hide in the corner of the kitchen and cover my head. My sister just sits there and starts to cry. Then my father yells, "What're ya cryin' for?" I see him reach for the fur whip behind the kitchen door. It's the only thing he seems to have got from being in the fur business. But Thelma gets to it first.

"Don't you dare raise a hand to my baby!" She is wild and screaming at the top of her lungs.

"Baby! Your baby! You're 'sposed to be producing a baby for me, and I don't see any results from you, you bitch!"

I run out of the kitchen and up the steps dragging my sister with me. I make her get in her pajamas and I get in mine. Then I put my head under my pillow to save my ears. My sister is not crying, just shaking. The fighting goes on for a long time. I hear water running in the bathroom and lots of muttering in the bedroom. At one point Thelma is crying really hard and I hear her shriek like she is hurting. I'm not sure what this all means. In the morning they are angrier than ever, and my father slams the door so hard when he leaves, the whole house shakes.

When I get ready for school, I try to stay out of my stepmother's way and just use water to smooth my hair from the day before. I put on socks without looking and don't even change my underwear. I put on a dress that feels too tight on me. I just want out of there. My stepmother is at the kitchen table smoking a cigarette like mad and working a crossword puzzle and swearing to herself. Barbara is eating a piece of toast with butter and jelly. When Thelma sees I have on two different socks, she grabs me by my braids and screams so hard, her spit runs onto my face.

"You troublemaker! You little slob! Look at you! You are making my life miserable." And without a pause she pushes her lit cigarette into my cheek. "I'll give you something to remember me by." I can't move. I feel my dress tear as I pull away.

I scream and my sister begins to cry. I want to kick my stepmother hard but I can't escape her hold of my hair. Instead I just go limp, and she lets go. I run out the door into the cold with no coat, no book bag, and no lunch or nickel. My face burns like fire and my pants I know are wet. But I never stop running even when I get to school. Inside, there's Miss Allison smiling and waving at me. *What am I going to tell her when I do not have my music book? What's she going to think?*

Miss Allison takes one look at my wet shoes and my dress with a big rip under the arm. Then she sees my face with a black round mark. Her eyes become wide and horrified. "My God, child, what has happened to you? Were you in a fight? Did a dog jump on you? Where's your coat? Should I call your mother?"

"I fell down a hill in the snow and lost all my stuff but I'm OK. Please don't call my...I do not want my m—m—other to know. She'll be very angry."

"Let's get you cleaned up." And she takes me into the teacher's room and washes my hands and takes off my wet socks. Then when she tries to touch my face, I cry out. She immediately takes me to the nurse.

The nurse looks at the top of my head, which now has a big scab, and then looks carefully at my face. They look at each other and say nothing. The nurse has me take off my dress and sews up the sleeve. Then carefully she re-braids my hair, cleans my face with something that burns, and puts some yellow stuff on my cheek and on my head. She gives me a brand new pair of panties from out of a cellophane bag in her desk drawer and rummages in the lost-and-found box for a pair of socks. I hang my head.

"Nothing to worry about, child," the nurse says. We'll just throw these others away." And she does. "Your parents do not need to know. This happens even to me sometimes. You must really have fallen very hard to get your head and face so banged up." I nod in agreement, half believing she is right and that my story is what truly happened. She takes an old coat out of the lost-and-found box. "Wear this home today. You can return it when you get your own coat. Lie down quietly on the cot in my office and rest for a while."

Then she and Miss Allison go into the hall and I can see them through the window on the door speaking quietly to each other and to my homeroom teacher. Miss Allison is dabbing her eyes and has her arms folded tightly across her chest. The nurse is shaking her head. The next thing I know, I wake up and school is out.

∾

Grandma becomes terrified when she sees my face. Aunt Elaine gets a phone call from the school nurse. Grandpa talks to my father in a loud and angry voice. My father swears up and down he did not touch me. And for once, that's true. But I do not say a word. My tongue freezes to the top of my mouth and my heart beats madly when my father makes the fur whip cut the air with a hum as he tries to find out if some boy tried to rape me. I'm not sure what that is. He sends me to my room, and I can hear Thelma and my father yelling and screaming and furniture breaking every which way. I hear the fur whip whirring in the air and feel its crack as it lands on the kitchen counter.

The next day I make sure when I get ready for school that my dress fits and my socks are correct, and I brush my hair and put the rubber bands on as best I can. My lunch is on the table—peanut butter and jelly for a change, and a dime instead of a nickel. I smile at my sister and pose in front of Thelma, hoping she will tell me I look OK. She doesn't say a word.

That day at school the nurse comes in and talks to the teacher and walks up and down the aisles looking at the children's work and saying how nice we are doing. She stops at my desk and pats my head real gentle and smiles at my face. "You look real pretty today, Shirley!"

I know she is trying to check on my cheek and on my head scab. But I am looking better, like Grandma says, "good as new." Everybody knows about my big time fall and they try to be helpful and speak real polite to me. Gracie isn't in school that day, but I walk home with another girl named Estelle. It puzzles me that the kids seem to like me just 'cause I got banged up and knocked around.

When I get to the house on Pittock Street, I see a lot of newspapers on the porch. I can see Mrs. Pasternak looking out her window as I climb the front steps. The door is usually open, but it doesn't unlock no matter how hard I jiggle the knob. I knock loud and ring the bell, but there is no answer. Then I put my hand over my eyes and try to see into the window. There is nothing in the living room or dining room—only newspapers on the floor and a sheet covering my father's chair from the apartment on Brushton Avenue. I go around to the back door, but it's closed tightly, too. Then I run over to Gracie's house.

"Mrs. Pasternak! Where's all the furniture? Where's my sister? Where's my ste—mother?"

"A moving truck came and took everything away first thing this morning. Your sister went, I believe, with Thelma. I'm not sure. I'm busy with Gracie today. She is not doing so good. I don't know what to tell you except to go to your grandma."

"Can I see Gracie?"

"No, not today. Maybe later this week." And she shuts the door very hard.

I try the doors one more time and even try to lift a window. I go to the garbage barrels in the backyard and see a cardboard box. There's my red and blue music books and my pome notebook ripped in two big pieces. I rescue the books and the pages and stuff them into my book bag. I look up and down the street for someone to help me. Across the street is Paul Mazerov all dressed up in his Boy Scout uniform. He is really handsome. I have wanted to speak to him about scouting and other things. He waves at me and calls my name. But instead I run up the hill to Phillips Avenue and to Grandma's house.

When I get there, my little sister is sitting at the kitchen table with a cup of milk and a sugar cookie in each hand. I'm so happy that she's OK and with Grandma, who immediately gives me instructions. "Your suitcase is at the bottom of the steps. Upstairs and change your clothes and into the tub! You look like you haven't had a bath in a week. Hair, too, please. Wash it good. Now, march!"

She has already put clothes on the bed. They are from my dresser in my bedroom on Pittock Street. That means that Thelma did not take the furniture that I got as a present for getting my tonsils out when I was nearly seven. And not another word is uttered. From all the *shushky*ing and Hungarian, I gather that Thelma has left my father, as my uncle says, "High and dry—bag and baggage!"

My father does not appear for days. He's still at the house on Pittock Street. Thelma left the beds for me and Barbara and took everything else she says she paid for. When my father appears again, he is white faced, and his mouth droops along with his eyes. He speaks to me so soft, he sounds like a ghost.

"We'll be back as a family soon, I promise."

He thinks that is just the right thing to say to me. It is the last thing in the world and my whole life that I want to hear.

I'm getting caught up on my missed schoolwork and am taking regular lessons from Miss Allison, which Uncle Sam decides to pay for. Grandpa sends me to Poale Zedeck Synagogue to Hebrew School, and I suddenly discover that my braids are good for pulling by some boy named Harvey, who sits behind me. He also annoys me in my class at school, which makes the other boys laugh. I have the job of walking Barbara to school. After school, Grandma picks her up at the Poale Zedeck and takes her the rest of the way. I walk home along with a bunch of other kids from the Hebrew School and am starting to get braver about having friends besides Gracie. She seems to be out sick a lot. Then Daddy's "soon" comes too quick to suit me. It is early in April and still pretty cold.

When I get home I see the suitcases out on the porch. My skin gets a furry feeling. At the kitchen table, Grandma is explaining to my sister about moving into a new apartment in the East End. "You'll live in a nice new place just two blocks from school on North Negley Avenue. Sorahlah? Do you hear what I'm telling your sister?"

"But, Grandma, why? We are doing just fine here. Why do we have to move again?"

"Your father and Thelma already moved everything a month ago. Your father is working for the Dravo Company in the shipyards."

I suddenly feel cramps in my stomach and a dry mouth. "But I need to be in school here. And how will I get my piano lessons? I'll miss the recital. Grandma, please. I want to live here with you, not with my stepmother."

"Sorahlah. Your father and Thelma are getting back together so that you can be a family. That is only right. You must learn to get along. You need to call her Mother. And besides, your aunt Elaine has to stay here while Hugo is learning his trade as a baker. Now go check the drawers and cupboard upstairs to make sure *du hast nicht fergesson anyting.*" Grandma did the packing so how could I forget anything? What's going on?

I can see Grandma wiping her eyes with the corner of a dish towel even though she turns away from me. She hardly ever speaks Yiddish to me anymore. I know she's suffering as much as I am. So I run up the steps and open the drawers. I become aware of the strong smell of cedar in the empty cupboard. When I bend on my knees to look under the bed, my stomach really cramps and I run to the bathroom. My pants feel damp and I hope I'm *not* having another accident. I gasp when I pull my pants down. There it is: a clump of bright red in the center of my underwear. Just like I heard the girls talking about having babies and giggling in the bathroom about falling off the roof and getting a little visitor and whispering in gym class about wearing what they call their training bras. Now I can brag that I got my period, too. And maybe get a training bra.

"Grandma! Grandma—please come here. I need you, quick."

Grandma comes bounding up the steps. "What's wrong? Are you sick?" When I show her my underwear, she looks at my excited, happy face and slaps that smile right off of it. I am in a state of shock. Then she grabs me and hugs me and kisses me, all smushy and crying.

"My Sorahlah, my *shaynical*! You are so young. Not even twelve yet. Oy! You are a woman."

She is happily hugging me and goes into her cupboard and brings out a brown paper wrapper. "Here, this is for you when you get the curse."

"Grandma, I know all about this from the girls at school. Why did you slap me?" Grandma has never ever laid a hand on me. Ever!

"It is what my mother did to me in the old country. It is a good tradition to be slapped." Then she takes my panties, washes them, and hangs them to dry. "You will have these when you come to visit again." She gives me a new pair out of her special drawer and runs down the steps when she hears my father's voice calling from the porch.

෴

North Negley Avenue is the very top floor of the apartment building—three flights up. The walls are freshly painted and the floors are all new linoleum. When we arrive, Thelma is in the kitchen running a wringer washer and dunking her hands in and out of the hot water. I can smell strong soap everywhere. My father puts our suitcases in the bedroom and tells us to fix up our drawers. I take charge and do my drawers and then Barbara's. I explore the bathroom. It has an old tub with claw feet, and there's a rust and blue mark around the faucet. The linoleum is not new, and there are a lot of cracks in the unpainted wall. The one light in the ceiling is a bulb that just hangs with a long chain on it. It reminds me of the bathroom with the ugly bugs. *God! I hope there's none here.* I shiver.

"Some nice place, huh, Shirley? I didn't finish the bathroom yet. But I need to wait for my next pay to buy stuff to fix it up." My father is satisfied with the place and Thelma is more affectionate to him. Seems they do what Uncle Sam says, like kiss and make up. But I am not going to count my chickens like Grandpa does as the *shoichet* in the chicken store.

"Shirley! I need you to help me take the baskets up to the roof to dry the curtains." Thelma piles lace curtains, sheets, and two of my father's white shirts into old bushel baskets from the fruit store. It takes two of us to get the first basket up the steps. Thelma already has a curtain stretcher up on the roof. I can feel the wind blowing up there as she shows me how to stretch the curtains from corner to corner and keep the hems straight. The stretcher has sharp, small, pointy pins to hold the curtains in place. I soon find my fingers bleeding and need an old dishrag to keep the blood off the curtains. We hang the sheets up end-to-end, and the cold wind flaps them hard, almost toppling the wooden poles that boost the clothesline high off the tar roof. I smell the Argo starch on the shirts and the Naptha soap. When Thelma lets me take up the next basket by myself, I enjoy hanging up the socks making sure the clothespins are tight. I can see way out over the neighborhood— down the big Negley hill to where the streetcars are stopping and over and across the rooftops. I can see the American flag flying high next to Rogers School. It begins to seem like an adventure in an unknown land just like *Dr. Doolittle* and *Gulliver.* I hope the library at the new school has lots of books and that I will find Miss Allison there just like I did at Colfax and Crescent.

When we sit down to supper, there's vegetable soup and sautéed chicken livers with onions. I'm feeling better about moving and going to a new school, although my stomach still is quivering at the thought. Well, at least there's only another couple of months to get through, and then the summer might be a time to have more fun or maybe go to Emma Kaufman Camp again. I'm even trying to talk myself into pleasing my stepmother and helping like I did today. Then Daddy taps his knife on a glass and clears his throat.

"I have a very important announcement to make. Your mother and I are happy to be here with you both in this new place and we are looking forward to a fresh beginning as a family. Right, Thel? So, it is time you know that you are going to have a new baby brother or sister come the new year. Isn't that wonderful?"

My stepmother and father exchange ecstatic looks and smile happily. My sister is not moved one way or another, and I just sit there and think about whether it is time to bring the sheets down so we can make our beds for the night. I am feeling awful tired. I haven't even been able to tell Thelma about my surprise visitor. I hope she doesn't want to slap me like Grandma.

Chapter Thirteen

IS YOU IS OR IS YOU AIN'T?
MAY 1944

Rogers School seems about the same as Colfax: same books, same library, same dumb gym suits! The teachers are different, but everything else's the same: chalk, books, and stale leftover cheese sandwiches from lunch. If you pay, you can get hot dogs and baked beans or macaroni and cheese. Not kosher, of course. I just sit with my sister at lunch and see that she eats OK and drinks her milk. There's no other Jewish kids, that's for certain. And my father makes sure that they use my real American name, Shirley, on the school records.

"Just keep your religion to yourself, you hear me? In this neighborhood, we don't need to look for trouble. The less you stand out, the better for the family. That goes for livin' in this tenement building, too. Don't get friendly or borrowing sugar or anything. Everybody needs their own food stamps what with the war effort."

It doesn't matter to me. They don't bother me and I don't bother them. No one is mean, but they don't much care. In Rogers School, there are a lot of colored kids, but they aren't so different from me. They stick to themselves, too. There's no gifted class at Rogers. We all do exactly the same work from the same books, and the boys throw paper airplanes and spitballs same as always when the teacher isn't looking. The teachers mostly give out workbooks, and you have to copy from the blackboard a lot or practice letters from the handwriting chart with a scratchy ink pen. That ink stuff is sure hard to get off your fingers. When my father asks me about school, I answer with my most used word, "Everything is the *same*."

I find out that Miss Allison does not come to this school, but they do have an orchestra if I want to play an instrument. My father says, "No money for lessons!" I can't get him to understand that the instruments are free.

"There's nothing for nothing!" He won't discuss it so no point in arguing!

When there's no chores or homework, I begin recopying my torn pomes in an extra composition book the homeroom teacher lets me have.

After school, Miss Graham asks me, "What do you want to put in this book, Shirley?"

"Uh, I need it for writing down my pomes."

"You mean your po-ems." The teacher laughs at the way I say the word. She makes the word real clear in two *sybalells*. "Can I see some of what you write?" Then she takes the torn book before I have a chance to say no. And her face gets a real big smile. "Why, Shirley, this po-em about the Amazon is very good. Would you like to read it aloud to the class during homeroom period? When did you write it? What school were you in before?"

"Uh, uh, I don't think so. Maybe when I get everything copied out better." I don't want to go into how at Colfax we did lots of creation learning. Worse, I can see my father's face if I stand up and start getting known in this school for reading poetry, which he thinks is just dumb stuff anyway.

"Well, perhaps when you are here longer, you will feel more comfortable getting up in front of the class. But I want to read all your poetry. Let me lend you my favorite book of poems. You will enjoy it, I'm sure." And she goes to the windowsill and hands me a book called *A Child's Garden of Verse*.

I'm really excited and smile at the teacher, who already has her coat and hat on. "Thank you so much! Bye, Miss Graham." I run down the steps to find my sister waiting by the door and practically skip all the way home, dragging my sister behind me.

When I look through the book at home, I see how a *po-em* is not written like a story and how some rhyme and some don't. *Why didn't I see that before? I write po-ems and they go into a book of verse. Now I kinda know how to say the word the right way.* This makes me feel good.

After we get home, Barbara tells Thelma that the teacher made me stay after school. "What's going on, young lady? You're not starting your late and complaining business again, are you?"

"No way! Miss Graham wants me to read po-ems in front of the class and she says I can do it when I'm ready." I can tell from Thelma's face that she is pleased.

"It's a good thing to read aloud in front of the class. Just make sure that you go over the words with me before you do it so you do not mispronounce anything. I don't want you to sound like an immigrant. That would upset your father."

That means reading a poem aloud in the class, like it or not! It surprises me that my stepmother will help me with anything. But starting at supper, as she begins correcting my speech and what she calls my grammar, I suddenly speak up. "You are real partikuh-lar about speech and use big words, huh?"

"Yes, absolutely! That's how I kept my important position with Reliance. Try to remember how to speak correctly. Say: really par-ti-qu-lar, and don't keep saying or ending a sentence with *huh!*" Thelma uses her knife in her hand to make the point.

My father smiles in approval. "Thelma was a big-time book-keeper and secretary at Reliance Steel Company in Altoona. She knows things like shorthand and how to write a real good letter. She's good with crossword puzzles, too. Shirley, I want you to learn business skills like your mother. She's gonna help me when I get my own business, huh, kiddo?" My father says this very loudly. Thelma doesn't correct my father's *huhs* ever, and she never mentions reading poetry again.

❧

Weekends are a relief from school. Because I don't use my milk money at lunch time, I save enough to go to the Enright Theater on Saturdays to see the movies and *The Kiddie Show*. It costs me a nickel for the streetcar and ten cents for the show. But then my father makes me take my sister along.

"Your sister can go free on the streetcar and here's a dime for the movie for her. Just make sure you hold her hand and watch out for any dirty old men." My father kinda whispers this like it's a secret. The only dirty men I see are cleaning down under the sidewalk or tearing up the bricks on the street. My father is plenty dirty when he comes home from the shipyards. His fingernails are all black, and Thelma gives him strong soap and a scrub brush to get them clean. The first time we go to get the streetcar, my father walks us down the hill to the corner. He waits and waves when we get on and find seats. "Don't talk to strangers and don't take no wooden nickels!" He laughs hard when he says that. I don't know why.

Thelma and my father are glad for us to leave them on Saturday. It's his only real day off, and they go shopping and just laze around the house. My stepmother packs us a lunch to eat at the movies since we stay for more than three hours: sandwiches—made from the chicken out of the soup we always have Friday night—on fresh *challah* with lettuce, pickles, and lots of mayonnaise. The smell from our brown bag is great, but other kids move away from us when we crunch those pickles. The first time we go, my sister is OK, sits still and listens, and is busy licking her fingers from the mayonnaise. She doesn't pay attention to the serials about cowboys and Indians. It seems I have to take her to the bathroom every time something good comes on the screen.

The second week she drops her sandwich on the floor and I end up giving her mine. Then she plays with the empty brown bag, which rattles and makes noise. People yell at us to keep quiet. When the new serial about *Mark of Zorro* comes on and the shooting begins, Barbara whines about how she wants to go home. I spend my own nickel and get her a candy bar, but nothing helps. It gets worse when *The Kiddie Show* begins and the microphone squeals. She starts bouncing up and down on the chair. When the kid behind kicks her chair so hard even I can feel it, my sister starts crying. The manager shines the flashlight in my face and says, "If you can't keep her quiet, you will have to leave!" He shines the flashlight right in my sister's eyes. Now she's crying even louder. I drag her up the aisle and out to the streetcar.

She doesn't stop crying even when we get to our own door. "What did you do to her?" my father demands. Thelma is busy wiping Barbara's face. I don't need to say anything. My sister sobs, "Somebody kicked me in the back and the movies are dark and a boogey men yelled at me and shined a bright light in my face and…" By that time, my stepmother is pouring her milk and giving her a slice of apple pie. After that, my father agrees that I can go by myself.

I love that! I get to sit through the serials two whole times and can watch the movie at least one and a half times. Gene Autry, Tarzan, and Zorro are my favorites! One Saturday they show *King Kong.* Usually, I make my lunch last through the entire movie, but that movie gets me so upset that I eat my whole chicken sandwich at once! After the theater shows previews of coming attractions with great love scenes of Spencer Tracy and Betty Davis and Joan Crawford and Jimmy Cagney, I decide that I want to be a great actress. But when *The Kiddie Show* is on, I imagine getting up and singing. *I wonder if I could get up on the stage like the other kids do and sing or play the piano? I could be a lot better than some of the ones up there.* I never get brave enough to ask my parents for permission to appear.

Riding the streetcar home, I get a real good idea! *Why not try out my singing voice in homeroom instead of reading poetry?* Miss Graham is pleased that I want to do it. She says I can do it on a Friday when homeroom has a kind of show and tell for older kids. I practice my song at home in the bathtub while I'm shampooing my hair. No one seems to notice with the water running, and I feel really good about my voice. I learn a song from the radio that is on the top hits list. Friday arrives. Other kids get up in class before me and tell stories about their family or read a book chapter or show a work of art or something. No one seems to care about anyone's performance. No applause, no anything—just lots of yawning. Then it's my turn.

"All right, Shirley, let's hear you sing." Miss Graham sits in my seat and smiles at me. She taps a ruler on the desk for the class to sit up and pay attention.

I get up all prepared and begin. "Is you is or is you ain't my baby…the way you're acting…" My hips and legs are doing a wiggle and a twist that goes with the song. My voice is loud and full of energy. My dress is swinging around. The class just screams with laughter. The boys hoot and suck their cheeks in, jump up and mimic me. I stop dead! Miss Graham is up and out of the chair and bangs the ruler on the desk. I feel my face get red and hot.

The teacher grabs me with one arm around my shoulders. "That will be enough, class." They all get real quiet except for a few snorts and snickers at the back of the room. "Shirley, you need not sing so loud or jump around and jiggle. Pick a more appropriate song next time." She is whispering, but everybody hears her. I sit down real hard and look at my desk. My stomach is full of terrible butterflies.

Miss Graham instructs the class on how to behave at a performance and makes everybody write one hundred times on lined paper, *I will be a polite listener!* Soon as the bell rings, everyone goes to the cloakroom for their coats and hats. I can barely look anyone in the face. The white girls all snicker when they look at me, and the white boys push their backsides out and wiggle their hips. The colored kids wave at me, and one colored boy whispers that he thinks I did real great with that Negro song. I just turn in the other direction. Miss Graham stops me before I leave the room.

"What made you pick such a raucous song? I don't think the class is ready for that kind of music. Ask the music teacher next time to help you choose a better piece. I can hear you have a nice voice."

Raucous? What does that mean? I shrug my shoulders and make for the stairwell. The colored kids are at the bottom of the steps laughing behind their hands. *They must think I'm a real jerk trying to sing a Negro song!*

"Hey, Shirl, girl! You got lots of voice and move real swell." It's the shortest colored kid in the school. He doesn't have any front teeth. I smile weakly when he makes a rhyme with my name. I rush to my sister, who is scuffing her shoes outside on the concrete steps. All the white kids from class are on the playground still wiggling their hips. *They're making fun of me. I don't wanna get up in class again to perform, ever.*

Chapter Fourteen

LUNCH AT THE MOVIES
1944 TO 1945

Once I learn to take the bus by myself, Saturdays at the Enright Theater are the best time of my whole week. I don't have to set the table or do homework or hang the laundry out on the roof. In the dark I can sit and just think about nothing and enjoy the chicken sandwich. It doesn't matter if I don't have a friend. In the movies I'm on my own. It's a good feeling to know how to do something all by myself.

Then one Saturday my father tells me, "Get a transfer when you pay your nickel. They'll let you get on the same number streetcar after the movie and go all the way to Squirrel Hill. Grandma wants you to visit for the weekend. Get off at Phillips and Murray and walk up the hill to Grandma's. You will stay overnight and come back late Sunday with Uncle Sam in his car."

I can hardly stand my excitement. Thelma helps me pack pajamas and a change of underwear, an extra blouse, and a toothbrush in the shopping bag right along with my lunch. I am so excited and grateful that I give her a big hug and an almost kiss. She does not hug me back.

I make my way down North Negley and get on the streetcar. The conductor gives me the transfer, which I stuff in my pocket. *It's funny remembering how I almost got lost when I went to the library by myself before my mother went away. I know how to read now and can ride a streetcar just fine.* I hardly know what the movie is about. When *The Kiddie Show* comes on, I don't pay attention. My mind is racing about getting on the streetcar and using the transfer.

Then the microphone squeaks as the announcer introduces a boy who starts singing. My ears perk up like a shot. *My god! He is singing my song, "Is you is or is you ain't my baby?" He's wiggling his hips and throwing his backside out. And he's a white boy!* The audience is yelling and screaming and jumping up and wiggling right along with him. *Is he from my class at school?* I can't recognize his face with the bright spotlight on him. But when the song ends, I jump up and applaud wildly, screaming along with everybody. I don't know why, but inside myself I feel great! My face is smiling so hard it actually starts to hurt. Suddenly, I get jerked out of my mood. *Whoa! The movie is going to start again. Get outside for the streetcar.* I rush out of the theater past all the parents picking up their kids. A lot of people are at the streetcar stop. I have to keep standing on my toes to see the number on the front of the streetcar. When the right one comes along, I get on and sit facing the front but keep looking out the side so I will get off at the right street. The transfer is wrinkled in my pocket. Lots of strangers appear on the streets. Stores whiz by faster than I can read the signs. People get off and on as the conductor calls the names of stops. *What if I missed my stop? Better go up and ask the conductor.*

Suddenly, the car jerks and goes dead. "Hold your seats! Nobody move. The overhead pole, the collector system is off again." The conductor instructs everybody and jumps off the streetcar; he steps carefully over the tracks. He takes a long pole attached to the side of the car and reaches up from the side to put the electric back on the wires that stretch way above the roof. I see sparks flying from the wire, and pretty soon he's back on the job, rings the bell, turns his seat around and we're clanging down the tracks again. I can see some sand flying from the front of the wheels. "Next stop is Forbes," he calls out. *I must have missed my stop.* I get up and holding onto the pole at the front of the car, I lean forward and speak.

"Mister, did we get to Squirrel Hill yet? I have to get off at Phillips."

"I'll call it," he smiles at me. "Just stay in your seat, missy."

It seems forever until the conductor yells, "Murray and Phillips Avenue, Squirrel Hill. Your stop, little girl." He presses his foot easily on the pedals that control the brakes. "Watch your step getting off. Don't step on the tracks."

He takes my transfer, and I am off the streetcar in familiar territory again. There's Hermann's Bakery and the deli and Phillips Avenue. And right on the corner is Grandma, standing, waiting. She hugs and kisses me. "Oy, my *shaynical*, my grown up girl." I hug her back. *How long has she been standing waiting for me?*

"Grandma, I brought my jammies."

"*Gut!*" She pokes around in the bag. "Phew, I think you brought me pickles, too."

Everything in the bag stinks from my lunch. It doesn't matter. I know Grandma will make it all right.

౭౨

Even though *Shabbes* is not over, Grandma washes my stinky clothes including what I'm wearing. She runs the shower for me and makes me wash my hair. The shower feels so good. On Negley Avenue we can't use the shower 'cause it's broken. We only get a bath two times a week, and there's never enough hot water so we each have to take our turn on a different night. It's my job to scrub the tub with Bon Ami real hard and wipe up the floor. I don't mind the scrubbing. It's the ugly big black bugs that run and hide in the walls that make me shiver. My father's not been able to fix it up or replace the linoleum. He is too busy working at Dravo's Neville Island Shipyard building LST's for the war overseas. "My pay," he says, "doesn't go very far." At Grandma's house, I don't have to clean the tub and I stand under the shower a long time at least until she yells, "*Genug!* We do not need to support the water company."

Grandma lays out the panties for me she keeps in a drawer along with the brown wrapped packages for anyone who gets the curse. She takes a new blue jumper dress out of the cupboard. She's been saving it as a surprise for me. It fits perfectly. It looks great with my clean blouse. After a light snack of a cheese pocket and some hot tea, I am to go with Grandpa to the Saturday night services. I am so happy to walk with him to the Poale Zedeck. I look forward to the smell of herring and the *challah* again.

Grandpa's voice sounds perfect! There is a large crowd of men on the first floor. But the balcony is practically empty. Where are all the women? When Grandpa sings the blessings on the *bima*, I rush down the steps so I can be first at the table. First or last, it does not matter. It looks like Old Mother Hubbard's cupboard—bare. There is wine that is really pale. As Grandma would say, "Who watered the wine?" *No herring! No* kichel*! No challah! Just some leftover honey cakes from last week's Bar Mitzvah—hard as a rock.* "What happened?" I ask Grandpa as we make our way home.

"The war has not helped the *shul.* We do not have a ration card. Everywhere there are cutbacks. The women are scraping by. Your grandma is amazing. She is making a lot out of a little and it always looks like more."

When we get to our own house, there is no cutback for sure. Freshly baked *challah,* stuffed *kishka* for Grandpa, kasha and bow ties for Uncle Sam, and no watered wine for sure. I'm allowed to sip a tiny bit after Grandpa sings the *broche.* And then, I really feel blessed, 'cause special for me, chicken soup with little square noodles and orange carrots with cut-up parsnip and celery swimming in the golden broth. *Mmmmm! Delicious.* After three whole bowls, most of which I just drink from the blue-edged china, I am ready for a nap. I don't even have enough room for the delicious nut rolls Grandma has put away in the back of the icebox. I want to ask her how she gets all this food on her ration card, but before I can open my mouth, she shoos me upstairs with a wave of her hand. "Sleep well, my *shaynical.* Tomorrow, you will go with Grandpa to Schenley Park to ride the merry-go-round like always."

I drag myself up the steps and find a lovely nightie full of flowers with little buttons at the neck. I notice it has the name of a girl I used to know in my class at Colfax sewed in the neck. This is what Thelma calls hand-me-downs. My father would die of embarrassment. Then I remember how Grandma picks the softer vegetables for a discount at Ross's Market and how she fattens up chickens in the basement. Grandpa always brings home the cow *kishka* from the slaughterhouse. We have an awful lot of noodles with everything. *But how is there always dessert and fresh challah?* Uncle Hugo,

Aunt Elaine's husband, is apprenticing at Hermann's Bakery. He appears every Saturday morning with a big bag of what he calls his mistakes. Everyone laughs. He goes home to Aunt Elaine with a shopping bag of leftovers from *Shabbes* dinner. Making a lot out of a little has become a way of life for the war effort in our family. I crawl under the soft feather *pairanah* full of goose down from Hungary, feeling warm and full and totally at home.

&

The next morning Uncle Sam shakes me awake. "Your father needs to talk to you on the phone right away." *My father wants to talk to me. What trouble am I in? What did I leave undone at home?* I practically tumble down the stairs.

"Oh, hi, Daddy. What? Oh, my! Yes, I understand. I'll tell Grandma. Oh, when you bring my sister, please put clothes in a suitcase for me…" But he is already gone from the other end of the phone. I rub my eyes and wander into the kitchen.

"Grandma, Daddy says I have to stay here at least two weeks and he is bringing Barbara later today."

"*Fer voos?* What is going on?"

"Thelma is bleeding. She lost the baby." I can only think about my mother and my other little sister in the long box. *Is that going to happen again?* I know that I will miss the last weeks at Rogers School. *Will I get put back?*

"Oy, yoy, yoy! Not a good thing. Shonyee, call him back and tell him to bring enough clothes *fer deh kinder*. Sorahlah, go get dressed before breakfast and tell Grandpa to hurry out of the bathroom. I need to go, too."

I bang on the bathroom door and give Grandpa a hurry-up call. Then I put on the jumper and blouse from yesterday. There's that label with another name again. I am happy to have something new to wear. It doesn't bother me. *I just hope I don't run into L. Gershuny on the street wearing her old clothes!*

For Sunday we have some of the nut rolls with tea and lots of butter and Grandpa has his usual eggs he cracks and eats with a spoon. Then we're ready to go down Phillips and up across to the other side, passing Davis School and lots of houses packed close together. The apartments are red and gray brick with windows open. A few ladies are busy shaking rugs or feather quilts out over the windows giving them a good snap. The air is filled with specks of dust and dancing feathers. The bushes in front of the building are covered with fading yellow forsythia, and the grass is just on the edge of turning green. People are sitting out on the steps reading their *Sun Telegraph* and *Press* newspapers. I can see some of them reading the funnies. It feels like spring is going to give way to summer soon.

Grandpa stops to talk to people who always seem to know him from the synagogue or the chicken store or the slaughterhouse. They refer to him as Reverend or Fischel or Rabbi. They always pat me on the head. Grandpa introduces me as his *ayenical*—his grandchild—*rosh kishlein* but *shayne vie goldt—a mix of Yiddish and Hungarian calling me a naughty girl but pretty as gold.* His teasing makes me blush. We make our way across Wightman Street past half houses and three-story apartments up lots of steps. When we get to Hobart Street, the houses begin to be larger with pointed roofs and open windows with lacy curtains blowing in the wind. A couple of houses have curved driveways with large, fancy cars parked in front of the door, and men with gray caps and buttoned-up tops leaning against them smoking cigarettes. "They are chauffeurs who drive the rich people living in those gigantic houses to work and everywhere," Grandpa explains. *No streetcars or transfers for them, I guess.*

As we get closer to the park, I can hear the music and the stop and start bells clanging. It's the merry-go-round. Some of the painted horses are moving up and down, and I spot my favorite one: a pure white horse, with legs curved up and a gold-painted mane and arched tail. Aunt Elaine says I'm too old to be riding a "carousel" with little kids, but it is one of my favorite things. I feel like Gene Autry at the Enright Theater. I climb on and grab the leather strap and start to smack the horse. It's great to pretend and not have to put up with the slobbering stinky smell of a real horse like the peddler man has.

Grandpa takes out a nickel for the man who has his hand on the big controller. "*Nein*, Fischel! For you it's free. You always make sure my wife has a chicken or a *bissel fleisch*. Call it a clergyman's discount!" The two of them laugh. I am not sure what a clergyman is, but it gets him a lotta stuff for free.

The bell clangs three times, and children jump on the lion or in the benches or grab a black or creamy colored horse. Most of the parents jump off and sit on the grass and eat a packed lunch and wave at their kids every time the carousel comes 'round again. Grandpa sits on a bench and reads his Jewish paper, *The Forward*. I know he enjoys this time by himself same as me. So I stay on again and again, going up and down and up and down. The music plays so different from a piano and makes me kinda sleepy and I get a little dizzy from staying on so long. I ask the control man why the sound is so echoey and tinkley. He explains how the music comes from a calliope with metal pieces and hammers and holes making the notes. I'm very ready to get off when two o'clock comes.

Grandpa grabs my hand when I jump off. I hold on tight till my legs can feel the ground again. The control man shuts down the music, picks up all the candy wrappers, and wipes all the sticky fingerprints off the horses. I watch as the lights, which flash off and on each time the music plays, go out. The carousel is dark.

Same as always, Grandpa buys me an ice cone in a paper cup from a man nearby with a red-striped cap on his head who pushes a glass cart with wheels. I ask for strawberry flavor—lots of it—and try to make the ice last all the way home. The sweet red syrup is a wonderful sugar treat. And it doesn't cost a ration stamp!

Chapter Fifteen

MOVING RIGHT ALONG
LATE SPRING 1945

My sister and I end up staying with Grandma and Grandpa for more than just a couple of weeks. It seems my father is making arrangements to move again—back to Squirrel Hill. Thelma feels they can't have a baby because the steps and climbing the hills and all the unpleasantness in the neighborhood makes it impossible. It's too late for me to transfer back again to Colfax school. For me it's great! I am happy living with my grandma.

In the meantime, while my father makes arrangement for a second floor duplex at 206 Wendover Place, I am busy practicing the piano at Mrs. Wolf's next door. My grandparents don't try to stop me at this point. Aunt Elaine pays for lessons I take with some-one my grandpa knows. That's at least until she and Hugo move to Detroit. Hugo writes my aunt love letters from Detroit every day, which she smells and then kisses and presses to her chest. They can hardly wait to be together again and want to have a baby as soon as possible.

I take the opportunity while Grandma is in a "let her do it mood" to sign up for Girl Scouts at Beth Shalom Synagogue on Beacon Street. Rabbi Rose's wife is in charge of the troop. Then when Mrs. Rose hears me singing along with the other Scouts, she tells me that I can sing in Cantor Adelsheim's Beth Shalom Choir if I try out for him. He happens to live right down the street from Grandma's, and I go sing for him. He says I will do fine and gives me the music and the information about rehearsals. Lucky for me, they are right after Scouts; I begin singing Saturday mornings. Grandpa has no idea where I go and Grandma says nothing about it. I know Grandpa would be very mad.

I'm very much alone in the choir and in Scouts as well. Making friends all over again is hard, hard, hard! My friend Gracie is very sick with some kind of blood problem. Grandma tells me not to bother her parents. I'm not sure if she's coming back to school. Gracie's a good friend and I want to help her, but that doesn't seem possible. At night when Grandma says the *Shema* with me, we both include a special prayer for Gracie.

When I'm up at Beth Shalom, there's a group of girls attending Hebrew and Sunday school. Grandpa wants me to start back at the Poale Zedeck, which is orthodox. Not my father! He wants to join the Beth Shalom, which is a conservative synagogue. My grandpa and father argue loudly about it. My father feels that I will attend Hebrew School at Beth Shalom once we move to Wendover Place. Grandpa gets very angry with my father. He wants the family to stay strictly orthodox. I stay far away from that argument.

Then, suddenly boom! I get invited to a boy-girl party for Morty Granowitz's birthday. I'm in a total state of shock. Two girls I know from Colfax and Wightman schools, Estelle and Lois, find out we are moving back and get Morty's mother to invite me to his party. He lives right on the corner of Wendover Place where we are moving. I am all dressed up in first-hand clothes—I check the label! Aunt Elaine manages to get a nice present for Morty at a discount from Frank & Seder's basement. But when Uncle Sam goes to drop me off, I tell him, "I'm scared to death! I hardly know what to do at a girl-boy party." He practically pushes me out of the car yelling "You'll figure it out. Don't be such a big baby." As it turns out, I am so uncomfortable being a guest that I end up helping in the kitchen for the whole party. The parents love me! Estelle and Lois and Morty are puzzled. Lois, however, is glad to see me again, and I know we will be friends when I go back to school in September for seventh grade at Taylor Allderdice High School. Believe it or not, I do finally play spin the bottle and I kiss a boy or he kisses me. I'm not sure which way since it's my first time.

With the move to Wendover Place, I start junior high school, and the kids who remember me from Colfax or from Morty's party wave hello. I even spot that handsome Boy Scout, Paul, who gives me a wink. He gives my tummy a different kind of butterfly. I find another friend named Marlene Goppman who lives on Wightman Street just a little way from our new apartment so we get to walk home after school together. Our most fun is stopping at Sol's Drugstore to buy a cherry Coke and maybe a red licorice braid or some other penny candy.

Thelma and my father are busy trying to fix up everything in the new apartment. Then he decides to start on the road selling jewelry out of his car again. They join the Beth Shalom at a special membership rate, and at the rabbi's urging, he finally signs me up for Hebrew school. Uncle Sam arranges for me to study piano with his latest girlfriend, Joan, who is a music graduate. Since my father is not putting out the cash, he doesn't make a fuss. She's no Miss Allison, that's for sure.

School becomes the center of my day. The classes are busy! I take cooking and sewing in home economics. We make macaroni and cheese, which I try out at home, and everyone raves at how good it is! From then on when we have a milk meal, I'm in charge of doing the macaroni dish. I also learn to use a sewing machine. It's not my happiest experience. We all make the same blue jumper and have to wear it to school in order to get a passing grade. What an embarrassment! My sewing is so crooked that Grandma has to practically rip it apart just to get it to hang straight. I nearly cry at how ugly it fits. But everyone else looks just as horrible and Grandma tells me I'm in good company.

My father looks at me in the jumper and says, "You look like you come from one of those poor orphanages, and soon as I get some dough, I'm gonna' fix up my girls right." I throw the jumper into the ragbag Thelma keeps in the basement.

Then I hear him discussing with Thelma the possibility of opening a small office for jewelry sales. They are saving every nickel and dime they can get their hands on. Thelma says she will help by being his secretary and bookie. This makes my father and uncle laugh. I don't get the joke as usual.

At the beginning of school, I discover that they have orchestra, choir, and special music and dance classes at Allderdice. You can take these classes without paying anything. I don't tell my father, who will lecture me on "nothing for nothing." They call them arts classes or extracurricular. Since I register late for school, everyone is already in some group. I sign up for harmony as a regular class, and since I love to sing, I go to the choir for extra credit with Miss Emma Steiner—the sister of the Miss Steiner from Colfax. But when I start to sing, she catches me chewing gum and makes me wear it on my nose for the whole class even while I'm singing. Then she yells at me for singing too loud and too high. "You sound like a steamboat whistle."

I copy my singing voice from listening to the Saturday radio program called *Saturday at the Opera*—singing along with the women's voices, pretending to sing the French or German words by making up my own version of the language. I enjoy that kind of sound. Miss Steiner does not. She shouts at me in front of the whole class, "You don't fit in. I hear you play the piano. You will be the accompanist instead. But no more chewing gum, understand?" *How did she find out I can play the piano?* By the next class, although I don't want to, I'm prepared to try and be her accompanist. It doesn't happen. As soon as I walk in the room she makes me open my mouth and checks to see if I have gum parked in my cheek. As if that isn't embarrassing enough, she criticizes my posture and makes me stand with a yardstick across my arms and over my back behind my head. I am frozen in this position in front of the room for the rest of the class period. She has her eye on me constantly. "Keep that yardstick over your arms! You must learn to stand up straight in this class." The students are silent. She has done this to other kids, too. I can't believe she has a fan club of students who claim, "Though she's hardhearted, she does a terrific job of training everyone to sound great!" Many kids want to be one of Miss Steiner's students in the "A" choir; it's a big-time honor. *Uh, uh, not for me! I have enough yelling at home. I don't need it at school. Forget going to the choir. She'll never miss me!*

I stick to harmony class and start learning to write down music notes and make up my own pieces in class. I love it! My head fills up with songs and sounds I never knew were in there. I participate and listen and learn about music. Miss Laura Ziegler, the teacher, really encourages me and says that I have relative pitch, which means I can pretty much play what I hear and be almost accurate. "Some students are able to listen and write down music exactly, which means they have absolute or perfect pitch," Miss Ziegler says. I am far from the perfect group. Oh, well!

Then I find out if I take modern or special dance class, I won't have to take gym class. The thought of not having to undress in front of the other girls and wear those dumb gym suits is too much to resist. I later realize that I will have to wear a leotard in dance class! Can't get away with all this undressing. Since I am still listed on the choir role, it also means I would have to drop music class. This is not what I want! I mention the whole problem to Miss Ziegler, especially about my bad experience with Miss Steiner in choir. She just nods and rolls her eyes and says, "Let me see what I can do."

Next thing I know, Miss Ziegler tells Miss Esther Long, one of the dance teachers, "Shirley can play the piano without looking at any music." Behind Miss Long's closed door, they are talking loudly. Waiting in the hall, I can hear part of the conversation. Miss Long wants me to be her dance accompanist. Miss Ziegler agrees. "Perhaps they will let her exchange choir for dance and also have it count as gym." My head is spinning! "We need to make this happen," Miss Long exclaims with great enthusiasm. Miss Ziegler comes out and takes me back to her office.

"We are going to see if we can fix it for you to take the courses you really need that will be helpful to you. Of course, we will have to get permission from the principal, Dr. McClymonds, "Miss Ziegler announces. My face drops. "Don't worry, Shirley, Miss Long and I will work on Dr. McClymonds. He'll realize you have so much talent that it's important for you to be in both music and dance."

At Colfax I did not pass the tests for the gifted classes. But now, suddenly, it seems I will be in special classes for music. The English teacher, Miss Hartz, also puts lots of comments on my papers and says I show real ability for writing. So much talent? Real ability? They're going to have a meeting about me! It doesn't seem possible.

The principal discusses the exception (as he calls it) with all the teachers. They agree it will be good for me to drop choir, stay in harmony, and pick up dance class. Best of all, I will not have to take gym, but will have to wear a leotard. *At the piano? I solve that problem by coming to school with the leotard under my regular clothes.* In dance class, I am encouraged to make up songs and music to fit what the dancers do with their bodies: to improvise. That's the easy part. Afterwards, it is a struggle to write down what I played instead of trusting my memory. That's the hard part. Lucky for me, Miss Ziegler shows me how to line up the clefs and use the key signatures. *I wonder if I can write a special piece for the dancers when they put on a show in the auditorium?* Miss Ziegler and Miss Long tell me first things first.

On top of my schoolwork, I still belong to Scouts and sing in the Beth Shalom choir on Saturdays. Then Grandpa finds out from the cantor I'm singing in the service. Quicker than quick, he makes it clear that no women should be singing the service. "*Nein! Nein!* Never." He tattles to my father.

My father yells plenty. "You are out of the choir, out of Scouts, and out of the *shul!* You are to come straight home from school. No side trips with the Goppman girl or spending my hard-earned money on Cokes and candy at Sol's Drugstore."

I'm pretty sure that Grandpa tattled to get back at my father because he joined the conservative instead of the orthodox *shul.*. Why do I have to take the punishment for what my father doesn't want to do for his father? What does my father have against me making friends and getting a snack like the other kids after school? What is really going on?

Daddy and Thelma are back to fighting again. And they fight a lot every time her curse happens. I need to figure this out so I don't always end up in the middle of family fights.

On top of all of this, my sister has to have her tonsils out! I remember when I had mine out; it hurt worse than hell! That's my big joke for my sister, who doesn't get the joke. Neither do I, but it makes my father laugh. Even the ice cream could never make up for the horrible smell of ether and the sore throat. And her luck, it happens just when Halloween comes. I use the extra money I still have from my old sock and decorate the bedroom with black cats, funny paper pumpkins, and witch pictures. I save some of my stash of candy for when she can swallow again. That makes my sister smile a little. I'm glad.

∽

At Allderdice I never want to be late for school or miss my classes. I write down lots of story ideas and poems like a water faucet constantly going. The best part is that no one from my family knows. I am afraid it will disappear like the Scouts and Hebrew School if one word gets out. I never even mention school to Grandpa, Grandma, or my aunt and uncle.

But when Beth Shalom decides to let girls have a Bat Mitzvah for the first time, Rabbi Rose convinces my father to let me participate. I'm almost thirteen like most of the girls. "It will be a group presentation and a great mitzvah for the family and the congregation." Persuasion is Rabbi Rose's business. My father wants to become a big *shul macher.* It doesn't take him long to agree.

"It's good for business," he tells Thelma.

The presentation is successful, and my father receives a lot of praise from the members of the Men's Club and the teachers for helping this happen. He smiles and orders a clock with Hebrew letters on the face instead of numbers for the *shul* to put up on the wall. This makes him even more of a *macher.*

Then the rabbi further insists that it is most important for me to continue Hebrew and Jewish studies and become a confirmand. My father says that the rabbi really twisted his arm, but he agrees. He makes sure I hear him. "You go to Sunday school and that's all. No foolin' around with boys or any other crap." Which, of course, means no singing in the choir or parties. I don't much care since I have such a lot of things going for me at school.

However, Uncle Sam who has now taken over paying for my piano lessons with his girlfriend Joan Kane, is using this arrangement to collect on money my father owes him. My father for some reason doesn't fuss like he usually does. When I bring this up to Grandma she just rolls her eyes and mumbles, "They are going to *finagle* a deal you can be sure of that," Then Uncle Sam tells my father "It's time you got her a piano of some sort! I know a way to help get a piano real cheap so she can a practice for her lessons with Joan." That really surprises me. *It must be part of the deal Grandma mentioned. I just hope it isn't a clackity one.* After that, to my amazement, he also talks to my father about letting me have a boy-girl party. He gives it to my father very loudly: "Don't be so stingy. She's gonna be thirteen. She should have a mixed party like everyone else." I suddenly figure out that Uncle Sam must've really felt bad for me when I got scared about going to Morty's birthday party. It's hard to believe that it's the same uncle who calls me names like 'tooth pick' and makes fun of my nose. Everyone starts ganging up on my father including Grandpa. My father calls it blackmail! I call it my good luck!

After Uncle Sam pins my father down about the party, I get to invite eight kids, four boys and four girls. But as it turns out I invite all the boys and girls who went to Morty Granowitz's party plus my cousins Sam and Marilyn Bass. Uncle Louie Bass brings my cousins early on the day of the party because he is doing plumbing work for my father. But then, for some reason, Uncle Louie and my father argue about paying for the repairs. Louie gets mad and makes my cousins leave before the party starts. They are disappointed and so am I, but Thelma tells me to be happy she let me invite more kids than Daddy said and especially my friend Gracie who is back in school. I keep quiet after that.

At the party all the kids (except my sister) play spin the bottle and wear a blindfold and grope around for each other, which annoys my father. We have Thelma's homemade banana cake and toasted almond fudge and French vanilla ice cream from Isaly's. It turns out to be a great day and I get some swell stuff. My stepmother's brother, Irving, and his wife, Yvette, take a picture of everybody sitting on the couch. When my sister cries, Estelle Olitsky lets Barbie sit on her lap so she can be in the picture, too. The best part is when my father tells me that a piano will be delivered as a birthday present sometime soon. I do not know how to take all this sudden attention and pleasantness. That night my father announces that Thelma is once again expecting. Somehow I don't think that's the end of the story.

෨

   The day of my party is the first time I get to see my cousins Sam and Marilyn after so long. I don't see Bubbie or Aunt Mayme at all. That's all I ever see of my mommy's family except every month or so when my father takes me to visit my uncle Abe Levitin, who still runs the Belmar Moving and Storage auction house where I got my clackity piano. He is my bubbie's brother. Uncle Abe and his wife, Minnie; their daughter, Betty; and her husband, Jack Levy, who's our family dentist, all live together on Highland Avenue in a big house with white pillars. The house is full of gold-painted furniture they call antiques, and my father tries to get Uncle Abe to let him sell some of the old jewelry Abe gets from house sales. He figures he can sell it out of the back of his car when he travels. It turns out that if he has a couple of sparklers—as he calls them— from Abe, he will make good money off of a man in Ohio that Uncle Sam knows. "This guy has a real thing for the old antique rings Abe picks up," my father tells Thelma. We usually make the trip over to Highland Avenue so my father can look over the possible merchandise.
   Each time we go to Uncle Abe's, it's like a mysterious adventure wandering among the satin-covered settees and the yellow-shaded lamps with fringe and crystal baubles on top. One of my favorite things is a hand-carved old man that Betty winds up; he whistles and turns his woodenhead back and forth. There's lots of doodads: a silver ring box shaped like a heart plays the wedding march, puffed up pillows with brocade and satin trim that no one's allowed to lean on, and a porcelain doll with real hair as blond as

the sun and a long blue satin dress with lace and ruffles. When I peek under the skirt, there are white ruffled pantaloons with beautiful pink ribbons on the edge. But I'm not allowed to touch any of those things.

"They are too valuable and irreplaceable!" Betty warns me. "I do not want a child worrying about breaking something unintentionally." She says this in a little childlike voice and ends it every time with a giggle. Cousin Betty and her husband Jack have no children and no worries. They live with Uncle Abe and Aunt Minnie while Jack is busy being the total family dentist.

That's the only thing that bothers me; he always wants to look in my mouth to check the fillings he put in, bragging at how beautiful his work is. I am happy when he's not around. It's enough to have to listen to him cracking jokes and singing out of tune when I'm a prisoner in his dentist chair as he fills my teeth at his office. Not only do the drill vibrations drive me crazy, but sitting in the chair with a bib on and my mouth wide open makes it impossible to do anything but grunt or *uh huh* his jokes. He gets louder as he drills and sometimes forgets to let me spit, and slobber runs down my chin. I frantically point with my covered hand at my face until he notices I am choking. "Sorry there, kiddo, you need to speak up so I can hear you!" *How could he possibly hear me over his singing and the drill buzzing?*

Fortunately for me, when we visit their house, most of the time he is in his downtown office cleaning teeth or making false teeth or drilling someone else's tooth which, he says, "is usually rotten to the root." I don't want to listen to him tell my father, "Too much candy is ruining her teeth and she needs to see me more frequently!" It is the one thing Daddy and I agree on. Daddy believes visiting the dentist is worthless, and he tries to finagle not having to pay Jack even with the special family discount. "Stay away from the candy and use your toothbrush. That's why you have all those gold fillings."

Right after my birthday, we make one of our trips to Highland Avenue, and Daddy takes great pride in letting Uncle Abe, Minnie, and Betty know that Thelma is expecting again. They're very pleased for him, but within two weeks, my Aunt Elaine announces that Thelma's pregnancy is false and she's just very late with her period. Now he has to untell everyone. My grandma lets him know it is bad luck to say something before you are sure it will happen. It's also the first time I realize that if you don't get your curse, you are pregnant. The girls at school are busy debating whether a boy could kiss you and make you pregnant. *Oh, my! What about the boy I kissed at my party?*

I wait for peace and quiet to disappear and my falling off the roof to happen.

∾

My father and stepmother start going downtown to set up a small jewelry business in a shared space in the Clark Building. Some Hungarian man named Lahtzee Friedman does jewelry repairs in the back half, and my father has a glass case with merchandise in the front. "All expensive *tchotskies*!" Grandpa says. That's what my father calls Uncle Sam's girlfriends. I don't get the connection. They just look like bright gold rings and wristwatches to me. At night my parents put their heads together over figures and lists of possible customers and finding out how and where to buy merchandise for a good wholesale price. My father quits working at the shipyard and travels selling jewelry out of the back of his trunk just like he did when we lived with Bubbie, except no more punch boards.

I am responsible for the usual cutting of salad, heating up what Thelma prepares early in the morning, and seeing that my sister gets to school. "Don't leave her until you see her go into the school!" Thelma warns. She packs the lunches for both of us at night and leaves milk money on the kitchen table. If Grandma can't get my sister, I pick her up on the way home.

The piano arrives two weeks later. It's a Betsy Ross Spinet—really a small piano but thank heavens it's not a clackity. It's brand new! It seems my father made a swap with that man in Ohio—a sparkler for the piano plus a bunch of cash. He is happy to get rid of the ring. Thelma is happy with most of the cash. Uncle Sam is happy to take "his cut," he says, "for getting the customer for my father." Suddenly I understand what "*finagle*" means to my father, Thelma and to my uncle. Who cares? I am happy to get a piano! My father insists that I play his favorite song, "Besame Mucho," right away. My uncle makes me play his favorite piece—the "Hungarian Dance." They are both pieces I learned off the radio. My piano teacher, Joan Kane, doesn't care about how I learn off the radio. She shows me scales and gives me a Bach piece to play on my own.

Miss Ziegler wants me to study composition with a man named T. Carl Whitmer at Pennsylvania College for Women and take piano lessons on the same day with a lady named Helene Welker. Since I don't have any money that doesn't seem possible no matter how many snacks or drinks of milk I do without. Miss Ziegler tells me that she will have a talk with Miss Welker, who is her friend. I do not say anything about Joan Kane.

Miss Ziegler arranges for me to go and meet Miss Welker one Saturday morning. My sister is staying with Grandma for the weekend so I don't have to worry about dragging her along. I leave early and manage to find my way to Woodland Road, which is in a fancy part of town—north of Forbes, everyone says. I walk a big distance from Wendover up Hobart to Shady Avenue, down past Forbes Street and across Wilkins and back down Shady, practically two miles. I cut through a long driveway and some fancy looking backyard with a swimming pool and gardens. It feels like I'm going through Alice's looking glass. Some of the houses look just like Uncle Abe's with white pillars. Then I pop out onto a winding road. A colored man is on his knees digging in the garden. I stop and ask him, "Can you tell me where the college is?"

"Right down there, missy." He points with his digging tool down the curve of the road.

"Is that where the music building is, too?" I crane my neck to try and look for a sign.

"Keep walkin'," he says. "Make a left at the curve past the tennis courts. Has a red brick wall 'round it. Better watch you don't go on nobody else's yard. You're trespassin', ya know."

"Oh, yes sir!" He gives a funny laugh. "Thanks, mister." I start down the road. I find the place and enter through a door with a sign above it: *Music Building.* It looks like an old kind of house with lots of windows. Inside the floors are part stone and part wood. There are sounds of instruments playing and piano scales going up and down like Miss Kane does on my spinet. The entry has big chairs and lots of books on shelves next to a large board with notices and signs. A high, clear voice is singing a piece I never heard before; it sounds like the opera music on the radio every Saturday afternoon. But my nose sure recognizes that familiar smell of books and chalk. I go from door to door reading the name beside it. Then there it is, *Helene Welker, Piano.* The door opens before I have a chance to knock.

"Yes, Mary Ann, I will see you again next week."

A girl in a circular skirt with a sweater passes by me. Her arms are full of music books. "Bye, Miss Welker," she smiles.

Then the teacher speaks to me. "Yes, may I help you?" Her voice is quieter than I ever thought a voice could be. She has on a gray dress with buttons up the front and a lace cut-out collar. A matching sweater covers her shoulders, and a pencil is in her hair knot on top of her head. She wears what my Aunt Elaine calls no-nonsense shoes with laces and has a pink hanky in her hand, which she tucks into her sleeve.

"I'm supposed to meet with you, uh, with Miss Welker at eleven a.m. Am I late?"

She quickly checks a small watch pinned to her dress. "Oh, my, no indeed. You are very much on time. You must be Shirley. Come in. please, and let's get acquainted."

And so we do. We talk about my music class and my family and why I want to study. Then she asks me to play a piece. I am not brave enough to try the Bach so I rush on through my version of the "Hungarian Dance." She asks how I learned that piece in particular, and when I tell her, "Off the radio," she takes out a book from a cupboard and shows me the same piece printed on regular music paper. The hundreds of notes and all the sharps and flats make my eyes bug out.

"It is wonderful that you can play so well without ever having seen the music. Laura Ziegler says that you have an excellent ear." She speaks about how I need to learn to read from the printed page as well as use my ears to learn something. "Did you bring any of your original music with you?" I show her a simple dance piece I wrote down for Miss Long and one that Miss Ziegler helped me get correctly. "Play them for me, please."

I play my two pieces and try to watch her reaction out of the corner of my eye. She nods and begins correcting my hand and finger positions explaining as she goes along. Then she takes out a notebook and writes down exercises I should be practicing. She is certainly different from Joan Kane. Miss Kane just talks and plays for me, especially if my uncle is watching. She never writes anything down, and then she expects me to do it just like her the next time. I never can.

"I expect that you will do these exercises every day in preparation for the next lesson." Miss Welker turns and faces me.

"The next lesson?" My eyes are bugging out. "Is this a lesson, already? But I don't have any money, Miss Welker. How will I pay you? I mean I am…"

She interrupts me. "Shirley, you are going to prepare for a scholarship audition, which will happen in the spring. Until then, you do not need to worry about paying me. We will apply the scholarship money to any lessons you take." *Scholarship? I tremble remembering Mommy's voice: "That means you don't have to pay…"* By my face, Miss Welker can tell that I do not know what to say. "What you need to do is promise to practice and listen to what I tell you to do." I just nod as she gives me instructions.

"I want you to take this book of Hutchinson Exercises and begin on page one. Please do the C scale; I will write it down. And here are some hand and finger positions I want you to practice." She hands me a book and shows me everything and writes it all in a notebook. We go over the exercises again and again until I am sure of what to do. Then she speaks about my own compositions. "I am going to speak to Dr. Whitmer about you and see if we can arrange for you to study with him as well as with me. He teaches a class for beginning composers on Saturdays in this building." She does not mention any money for paying him either. Before I know it, the hour is up.

I am so filled with excitement that I throw my arms around her and thank her over and over. She reminds me, "Practice and attend to your lessons. I look forward to seeing you again in two weeks from today at the same time. Every two weeks is plenty for now."

When I go into the hallway, I see that students are gathering on folding chairs in front of a small stage in a large room. Miss Welker is going into the room.

"There is a student recital today. You are welcome to stay if you like."

"I need to get home, but thank you for asking me." I try to make my voice soft and refined like hers. Her voice echoes in my head, so different from my family.

I stop and read the board with all the signs. There is the announcement of this recital and other music things that happen at the school and at places called Syria Mosque, The Nixon Theater, The Stanley, and The Pittsburgh Playhouse. Places I do not know about. Places where making music is more than just listening to the radio. I read the words *Opera and Symphony Performances this week!* I make my way back up Woodlawn Road, holding on to my exercise books and filling up with butterflies beyond butterflies. I begin to feel ready to study like never before. But I know I will have to figure out how to handle lessons from Miss Kane and Miss Welker at the same time.

Chapter Sixteen

THE CHOCOLATE BAR
1945 TO 1946

Every time I eat a chocolate candy bar, I think of Raitzu.

Grandma's lips are trembling when she tells my grandfather loudly, "I will bring her here to us—after what she's gone through—such terrible things. I will find the money. She is my sister's child!"

She takes up a collection from her pinochle group, cajoling and wiping her eyes with a handkerchief. All have lost family in the war. It doesn't take much to get her friends to open their change purses. She counts the stash bundled in the same damp handkerchief she pins inside her dress to her white knitted undershirt. For weeks, Grandma gathers money from every possible charity *pushkie*—shaking coins out of the can no matter what the label.

"For my sister's child. I will pay it back," she declares without apology.

One rainy Thursday morning in March when the lingering chill of winter leaves a foggy mist around the streetlights, she enters our lives and "here" becomes now. I am staying with my grandparents for a long spring vacation, when I find her sitting on a straight-backed chair, eyes glued to the floor, her hands clasping and unclasping. As her feet rub across a bare spot on the carpet, she silently pulls her gray sweater sleeve over her knuckles. Her slightly curved body shivers. She seems like an ash tree without leaves, arms floating like slim willowed branches loosely at her sides. Her skin is pale, smooth—pulled across the bridge of her nose and high arched cheekbones. When she glances up quickly, her eyes look like empty black pools.

"Want some? Chocolate?"

I stand in front of this relative stretching out a chocolate bar. She does not look up at me—does not reach out. I put it in her hand, but it falls into the lap of her flowered dress. Her trembling fingers pick it up, and she gives it back to me still keeping her eyes lowered. I notice for the first time a twitch of her lips. But even bending down and trying to see her face, I cannot tell if it is a smile.

"My grandma says you are part of our family. Where will you sleep?"

Her shoulders shrug an unknowing silent answer.

"What terrible things happened to you?"

She shakes her head at this twelve-year-old *nebshit* but does not respond. I push the chocolate back into her hands awkwardly, waiting for some sound. She sits twisting her dress and mutters words that have no meaning for me as mine have none for her, spare as she is spare, empty as she is empty. Loneliness and anguish fill her face. Her fingers run across the brown wrapper of the candy bar. She holds it to her nose and inhales soundlessly. I do not know how to make her understand my words.

My grandmother feeds her soup and bread and a piece of banana. She tries to take the chocolate bar away from her.

"*Nein, nein,* Sorahlah! No candy. It will make her sick."

Grandma rolls her eyes at me. But this sad, wizened girl clasps my chocolate bar close to her chest and glances at me. Is it a smile?

"Yoy, her hair is so thin, orphans hanging over her ears and falling in her face."

Aunt Elaine helps Raitzu comb her hair and fixes it up with two bobby pins on each side. "There, that's better. A true Romanesque profile." My aunt smiles.

"Gut, now we can see your lovely face...a narrow chin like your mother's. Oy, yoy, my poor sister." Grandma's eyes fill with tears.

Raitzu slumps and I can see how rounded her shoulders are. We will share a bed; she will wear Grandma's nightgown. I give her my tooth powder and a new toothbrush; I show her how to gargle with salt water. She gags and spits up her dinner in the toilet. Her embarrassment shows as I give her a towel to clean her face. She timidly follows me into my bedroom. She fingers the nightgown as she stretches it over her head.

"Don't you want to take off your underwear first?" I know she does not understand me. "Why are there numbers on your arm?" I run my fingers across her forearm. She is alarmed and jumps into bed burying her face beneath the feather quilt and huddles closer to the wall. I climb into my side and pull the comforter across my shoulders.

"Good night, Raitzu." She is stiff and unmoving.

Her world is in one drawer. She keeps it tightly closed. But I know there are cotton undershirts, panties, and white socks Grandma has managed to gather along with a few hand-me-down blouses and skirts. There is even a new dress with a belt from her pinochle friends and a scuffed pair of shoes from my aunt's collection of footwear in the cupboard. I watch her finger the clothes and hold them up in front of the mirror, and once again, she has a ghostly curve on her lips. I see now that she has buds that bloom on her chest and she speaks in whispers with Grandma, who hands her a brown paper bag with the usual thick white pads. At night she opens her drawer and nibbles silently like a hungry squirrel.

Grandma keeps her busy peeling potatoes and washing the celery for the endless pots of soup we seem to be having for dinner. Raitzu's eyes fill with tears when she peels the onions. Sometimes I see her crying when she tastes the chicken soup and there are no onions getting peeled. Grandma chatters in Hungarian; she responds quickly. I try to translate, but the family likes to keep me ignorant so they can speak without my knowing what they are saying.

"Her family was taken from Budapest," Grandma tells me. "She remembers her Hungarian and Yiddish, and she speaks German from the camp. She is a very smart girl, my sister's child. Oy, oy…" and she hugs me tightly as her voice trails off in hard gulps. My hair gets damp. I cannot understand what the camp is. No one in the family will talk about it. "Better you shouldn't know," is Grandma's response.

I use my hands to talk to Raitzu going slowly along with my English. Every day I try to speak to her. Then one night as she comes out of the bathroom and climbs over me to her side of the bed, I hear her.

"*Gutte—nacht*...uh, uh, goot night, Sorahlah. *Danke*—tanks, please." I know for sure she is smiling.

Each time I visit, I teach her how to write her name in English, painstakingly using lined paper and showing her each letter. She nods her head excitedly and utters, "Tanks, tanks you so much." She smiles a lot now.

Grandpa begins to not smile so much. He shows Grandma figures on the back of an envelope. "We cannot do it, *Onyoukah*," Grandpa sternly admonishes. "Too long here; it is *genich*—enough." Then a barrage of Hungarian mixed with Yiddish rises loudly. "Enough is enough! That is the final word from me." Grandpa is determined to win.

I know that things will change. Grandma explains more to Raitzu in Hungarian. Her pinochle friends shake their heads. I do not understand. But Raitzu's face grows pale and one night, I hear her soft sobs and try to pat her back. She pulls away. Her stiff body returns. She no longer tries to speak English with me.

Two weeks later a letter arrives from Brooklyn. It is in English. Aunt Elaine reads the handwriting aloud for Grandma. "Grandpa has arranged for Raitzu to meet Schmuel from his side of the family. That will be good! Schmuel will take care of you; he is a kind man." My aunt gives Raitzu a hug. But Grandma is trying hard not to cry. I hear those same loud gulps as she turns away from Raitzu. All the rest is in Hungarian. I am not sure what is going to happen. I decide to stay over that night.

At dawn, before I am awake, Raitzu is put on the train with all her clothes in a black suitcase. I look into the drawer Raitzu used. The candy bar paper lies open—one tiny crumb and the smell of chocolate is all that is left. I sleep on my side of the bed and use the sheet to wipe my eyes.

Six months later when I am visiting Grandma again, my aunt reads us a letter from Schmuel. "I am grateful and thank you for caring for my lovely wife. She speaks English better now, but the first thing she wanted to learn was how to ask for a chocolate bar in English. We are very contented together."

My aunt asks me why I am smiling so hard. I just shake my head.

Grandma is pinning a lot of paper money to her undershirt. "For my brother and his two sons after all they have suffered! I will bring them here."

Two boys in my bed? Not with my grandma around. No way. I will probably be sent to the daybed in Grandpa's room when I visit. I begin saving my stash of chocolate bars.

I wonder if they will have numbers on their arms, too?

Chapter Seventeen

RUBBING SALT IN THE WOUND
APRIL 1946

Just as we are getting settled on Wendover Place and I have my routine down as to when I have to sit for my sister or practice or take lessons, a new issue suddenly appears. My parents hear about a sheriff sale for a single house on Melvin Street. I can hear them excitedly talking in the evening to their friend, Dr. Hyman Canter, and to my uncle. Grandpa puts his two cents in even though he is told to mind his own business.

"You have just got your feet wet in a new business," my grandfather warns.

"You owe money everywhere for that and two moves in less than a year! How can you afford to move again and carry a mortgage on top of it?" Of course, he is referring to money owed Grandma, who has forked over two hundred dollars. Uncle Sam reached into his pockets as well. And Dr. Canter, who I find out attended my mother when she died having the baby, offers to help him out, too. Dr. Canter feels obligated for some reason to my father. All this information makes me feel uneasy. But my father is determined to do this. "It's once in a lifetime," he says. Early on the next Sunday, we all take a ride down to see the property at 5659 Melvin Street.

My father exclaims, "It has a front porch and a garage in the back—a little hilly but a good sized piece of ground. I'll build a barbecue back there."

"There are three bedrooms and a full bathroom with a shower," Thelma adds. "The kitchen needs some work, but we will get to it. And there is a large dining room which can seat a lot of company." Both of them obviously want this house.

My father points out, "The two sisters will share a bedroom and leave the third bedroom for guests or hopefully soon for the new baby."

Grandma shakes a finger at him, making three spitting sounds out over her left shoulder. He ignores her.

"This house has a full basement so that the laundry will be only one flight down, and there is plenty of yard space to hang outside and the floor plan shows a living room with a nice staircase and a large white marble fireplace." We are all busy nodding and *uh-huh*ing. I have to admit from the outside it looks a lot better than any place we lived so far. So I vote enthusiastically for the house even though nobody asks my opinion.

Thelma hurries to add, "There's one thing about this move that is certainly good for me and Irv. I have yet to unpack all the boxes from the last move, and Uncle Abe is willing to let us move for free with his Belmar Moving and Storage Company."

But the tough thing is (I find out from listening to some lawyer giving advice to my parents one night around the kitchen table), "You will have to come up with the cash to buy on a sheriff sale and be high bidder to get the property. You will also have to be able to get out of the lease on Wendover Place."

I don't know what all the details mean, but somehow my father comes up with the right bid and all the money! And before I can hardly change my address card at school, we are piling our stuff into Uncle Abe's truck and moving. The colored man who moved my first clackity piano for me is one of the movers, and he smiles real big when he sees me and gives me an OK sign with his fingers as he covers my new piano and hoists it onto the truck.

Once we are moved in, Allderdice is about one-half mile closer to walk. Great for me! And since I have to make sure my sister gets to Davis School, I find a shortcut through the new neighbor's backyard that goes straight through to Phillips Avenue where the crossing guard is. Then after about six weeks, Barbara proudly negotiates the shortcut all by herself. Best of all, for me, there will be no new friends from scratch. My friends Marlene and Lois live pretty close by. And then in Confirmation class, I meet a girl named Patty

Goldberg who lives practically around the corner from Melvin Street on Hempstead Road. She's at Taylor Allderdice, too. We hit it off right away and have a lot to talk about and share more than any person before in my life. She is glad to meet me since she comes from Oil City and doesn't know anyone yet here at Allderdice.

We both love music and appreciate how hard it is to be from another place. She encourages me right away to study so I can learn everything there is about composition and singing and piano. She likes English class like me, and we share poetry and talk to each other about our schoolwork. H. Patricia Goldberg is her formal name, and I tease her a lot about it. It makes her mad but then she laughs about it. She teases me about my many names, too. Sorahlah, Sorah, Sor, Shirley Ruth, and sometimes by mistake—Sarah. That's when I know we are going to be more than just walk-home friends. Best of all, she is the smartest girl in the class and learns really quick how to get around some of the social snobs better than me.

"This is a strange group of girls! Noses in the air about anybody who doesn't measure up in their opinions," Patty claims. But she can put her nose in the air with the best of them.

What's more exciting is that once Patty and I become close friends, she encourages me to begin making my idea of a talent show at school happen. She helps me write up the idea and try to get permission from the activities director and the principal. It seems that the school is not in favor of it for this year, but "maybe next spring," they say.

"A full year and a half away!" I moan.

Patty's mother tells me, "You have enough on your plate for right now—both of you."

So since I'm just learning how to write and becoming better at accompanying and improvising, I do what my Uncle Sam tells all his girlfriends, "Just keep your lace undies on." Of course, I am still wearing plain old cotton panties and undershirts. Grandma makes sure and checks me all the time. Patty agrees that I really need to get a bra, but my parents do not see the need for one.

"What, on those little dimples?" my father laughs.

ᥫᩣ

This is the first time in my life that I am happy about moving! *I hope this will be better than the other times when there was so much yelling and misery and black uglies crawling around.* Of course, now Thelma has to go to work in the jewelry store every day, and my father is, as he says, "bustin' his butt on the road." But as Thelma tells Aunt Elaine on the phone, "We are determined to make a go of it."

Of course, there are added jobs for me to do with this new house. The big steel garbage barrels in the backyard next to the garage need to be hosed every week and lined with newspaper—my job. Not so bad except for millions of white worms my father calls maggots almost as bad as black uglies. I try to get rid of them and throw Clorox in the cans before I put in the paper. But no help! Next week, same sickening worms, which make me gag. I also drag the laundry up the basement stairs and hang out the clothes since Thelma is still trying to carry a baby. But there doesn't seem to be the horrible fighting or breaking of dishes in this house. Maybe it's the new neighbors who welcome us and pitch in to help.

As soon as we move in and barely have the furniture in place, some people on the street knock on the door bringing cookies or even a special dinner. For me, the best visitors of all are the Wolfs. The first day we arrive, there is my friend Miltie waving frantically at me three doors up! My heart is so happy that my friend who happens to be a boy is not even, as Grandma says, "a hop and a skip away." Thelma and my father are pleased with the great cookies his mother brings along with a large casserole; the boy-girl problem never comes up. The next-door neighbors, the Reingolds, are friendly and bring us a home-baked cake. They have a daughter named Benita but everyone calls her Bunny. She likes music and always has a happy hello and smile on her face for me. I hope that we will be friends even though she is younger than me. I feel that this is a great new beginning for us as a family.

Up the street are people named Al and Anne Klein. One of the best moments is when my father joins a poker group on the street courtesy of Al; Thelma plays mah jong with Anne Klein and a few of the other wives. She and Anne exchange recipes and visit back and forth. It's new to me that my stepmother wants girlfriends just like me. My father feels he is getting some respect for his new position as a business owner and passes out his business cards to everyone in the congregation and on the street. "Business is slowly picking up, and even though there's some pinching of pennies to pay back the loans, we are managing," he tells Hymie Canter. My father is more pleased with life in general although I know that they are still trying hard to have another baby.

He especially tries to butter up the Halperns across the street. "George is in the money," my father declares. Thelma and George's wife, Lillian Halpern, talk mostly about cooking. But all that Mrs. Halpern wants to chatter about is her daughter. "You know, Doreen is in Miss Steiner's "A" choir! Doreen has a remarkable voice. Doreen studies with a great teacher. Doreen has real nice sorority friends…" and on and on. They live right next to the Kleins, who also have a daughter named Harriet, who is a sorority girl.

My friend Lois's mother calls the sorority group *cliques*. So Lois tells a bunch of us at lunch one day, "Let's make our own clique!" And we do. The next week we are all wearing plaid ribbons on our sweaters and calling ourselves "the plaids." At first it seems a real neat thing to do, but the plaids last about two weeks total. In spite of the cliques and "A" choir, I get along just fine with the girls on Melvin Street.

Three months after we move, we get a visit from Uncle Abe, Aunt Minnie, Betty, and Jack who ooh and ah over the house and the coconut cream pie Thelma serves up. Uncle Abe gives my father a beautiful porcelain statue from one of his auctions. It gets an honored place on the marble mantelpiece. And then late one Sunday evening, without any warning, my grandmother's cousins, Bertha and Willie Hofstadter, pop in. They are recently arrived immigrants, and with my grandfather's help, Willie is applying to be the cantor at the Shaare Torah Synagogue.

In walks Willie, a yellow straw hat on his head, and Bertha in front of him all smiles, her front gold tooth sparkling. Her hair is rolled like hotdogs around her head. "We vant you should haf lots of *nachus* from a beautiful house and with your lufly family!" Her voice is in her nose, which irritates me a lot. And with that announcement she takes a brown grocery bag from under her arm and spreads salt over the newly polished hardwood living room floor including the rug and furniture. "This is *zalts* for goot luck and to vish you a healtee new baby to be." Willie's face lights up with a smile showing pointed teeth framed by a pencil thin moustache. He just nods in agreement.

Thelma's face is enough to paralyze Bertha on the spot. My father's mouth drops in total shock and his face is white. My sister and I, who are in our pajamas ready for bed make a run for the stairs slipping on the salt.

"Uh, huh, well—thanks for your gift of salt—but it's a little late and we are going to bed." My father is controlling his temper. But his face is beet red.

Bertha laughs. "Ach! Vie shoult call first, but vie are looking to move onto street here. Vie see tonight a triple maybe whole block avay. We are excitement to know cousins here." Then I hear voices muffling and the door slamming, and all the first floor goes dark.

"How can they know that you are pregnant?" my father yells at Thelma. These new relatives are not welcome, that's for sure. My father gets my grandma on the phone and lets her know right off how ignorant her cousins are. "They better not show their faces around me anymore."

Grandma is yelling on the other end. "He is a religious man. Treat him with respect, Vroomie." I can hear every word.

That does it! That is the childhood name my father hates. He bangs the receiver down. Thelma begins weeping and moaning about the furniture and the floors.

My father is beyond reasoning. "Forget the salt. You'll take care of it tomorrow when you get home from the store. I have to be on the road by six a.m. I'm beat. Upstairs, now!" My father is out of patience. And when Thelma continues crying, he starts to scream for the first time since we moved into the new house.

"I'm working my ass off and sweating blood and you are bawling about fucking furniture and floors. Worry about producing a son for me for a change. I want you in to see Hymie Canter pronto—this week. There's something you're doing wrong, bleeding my babies away."

I hear Thelma most of the night in the bathroom gulping and blowing her nose. I whisper to my sister, "Tomorrow come straight home; don't wait for me. I need to do something."

The next day I come straight home from school even though there is a special dance rehearsal for a program and get down on my hands and knees and clean up the mess. I re-wax the floor and polish all the furniture and mirrors and windows.

My stepmother comes in the side door and starts rattling pots and pans and frying up onions and liver for dinner. She sets me to mashing the potatoes and setting the table. She pulls out the vacuum cleaner from the back hall and lugs it to the living room. Then I hear her gasp. "What's going on? The mess is…"

I timidly come into the room. "I wanted it to be perfect the way you like it."

"The floors look brand new. Even the furniture is sparkling. Amazing."

My father walks in, and the first thing Thelma says is, "Shirley did a wonderful job! Look at this house! Spotless."

He nods and takes off his tie and hangs it as usual on the stair rail along with his jacket. "What's for dinner?"

Chapter Eighteen

BACH FOR DESSERT
MAY 1946

"Sit up straight, Shirley. Watch your hands! Stop swinging your feet. Ouch! That is the same note I corrected before. Can't you remember anything?" Joan Kane is giving me my piano lesson after Sunday dinner. Grandma, Grandpa, Uncle Sam and Aunt Elaine are busy listening. She yells at me for every little thing, and I can hardly get my hands to do what my ears and eyes tell me. Daddy doesn't like her music choices, especially Bach, which I am learning for the first time.

"Why can't she play something I know?" my father shouts over the piano and over Miss Kane.

"Quit complaining! What do you want? It's not costing you anything. Joan is being most generous teaching her for free." My uncle ogles his *latest paramour*, which is what my Aunt calls her.

Aunt Elaine gets her two cents in. "Seems she played better before these lessons."

Miss Kane points with a pencil at the book on the piano. "That's because she played mostly by ear, but she really couldn't read well. I am forcing her to read the notes. But she is a most intractable child. Now do that again, please, young lady."

Well, I think to myself—*intrac-ta what? That's a new word to look up in the dictionary. But I can't spell it.*

"Shirley! How about giving a hand with the dishes? I can't stand on my feet much more." Dinner is over and I can hear my stepmother, Thelma, banging pots and pans and running water in the kitchen while she yells for me.

I take the opportunity to leave the piano. "I need to help with the dishes."

My uncle yells over his shoulder. "Not until the lesson is over, Thelma. Now, Joan, begin again! I intend to get my money's worth."

"I am sure, dear brother, you are getting more than your money's worth. Hey, Thelma, where's the apple pie? You promised me pie for dessert." Daddy is big on dessert.

"That was before I had to go to the hospital again yesterday. It's enough there's dinner on the table!"

My father doesn't seem to care about that. "Stop your moanin'. That's why I married you. And for *crissakes*, get some clothes on. I can't stand you walkin' around in that wrapper. What are people gonna' think if they see you lookin' that way? The girls in my life gotta look like they belong to an up and comin' businessman."

Thelma yells back, "I can't cook and serve everyone dressed up like Mrs. Astor's pet horse."

Uncle Sam roars with laughter. "You tell him, Thelma! Make her play that piece right, Joan. C'mon, baby brother, how 'bout a hot game of gin?" Uncle Sam pulls out a deck of cards from his pocket. They pull the tablecloth back to make room for the game.

Aunt Elaine speaks up. "I'll give you a hand, Thelma. You shouldn't be on your feet after your miss last week."

"Miss? What's a miss?" I seem to be learning all kinds of new words today.

Grandma whispers to me, "She can't seem to carry past two and a half months. Third time since they got married."

Grandpa is horrified. "Shah! Don't speak of such personal things in front of me."

Grandma is annoyed. "Ach! A waste of time," and she gives Grandpa a real dirty look. "Play, Sorahlah, darling, you are getting better."

I begin the piece again for the umpteenth time as Joan Kane counts, "One, two, and play." I make the same dumb mistakes again. Joan's eyes roll around and she is really getting impatient with me.

"Oops! Sorry, Miss Kane. I'll try again."

But Joan Kane gets angrier as I make another mistake. She smacks my hands with a pencil. I jump up and bang the keys loudly. "I won't study with her. I won't. I won't! I want to take lessons from the teacher Miss Allison recommended at P-C-W."

Grandma is confused. "P C what?"

"P-C-W—on Woodland Road." I have been looking to manage the change of teachers for weeks now.

Grandma is alarmed. "Is that like the CIO or AFL—or *Gott*—a communist group? I hear lots of communists live on Woodland Road. *Apoukah, nem tudem, nem tudem.*"

Grandpa is even more out of it. "*Nem tudem*—I don't know anything either about lessons mit communists or…"

Given the opportunity, I take it quickly. "Speak English, all of you! It's a college for girls and they teach music. Musicians aren't communists."

My father turns on me. "No, but they're all queer. You're not going where there are queers, not even over my dead body."

Joan Kane is angry and turns her back on everyone wildly tapping her foot.

Uncle Sam has yet another opinion. "It's the richy bitchie side of town. No communists there, you can be sure. Joan Kane is the best teacher for her; she knows her music. And besides, brother dear, that's how I'm collecting on your debt. Be grateful for small favors."

Aunt Elaine comes out of the kitchen drying a pot. "But, Sorahlah, that's on the other side of Forbes! You couldn't get there."

"I can walk!" I'm getting braver, hinting at what is really going on.

"Where would the money come from? Even with me in Irving's store every day, we don't have a spare nickel." Thelma is at least practical.

My grandma winces when Thelma uses my father's new name.

Uncle Sam jumps out of his chair. "Gin! After this game you won't have a plugged nickel."

"I can get a scholarship…"

I haven't finished my sentence when Miss Kane turns in fury, waves her arms and blurts out, "Scholarship? Scholarship? Hah! Based on what repertoire? You can't even play the first simple Bach piece."

"Miss Long, uh, I mean, Miss Allison says that Miss Welker at PC—Pennsylvania College for Women will get me ready."

"That—is an impossibility. No one could get you ready." Miss Kane puts away her pencil and notebook.

"Look here, Miss Cohen…" My aunt is now annoyed.

"Kane, my name is Kane—Joan Kane, if you don't mind."

"Don't get so fancy schmancy. I remember you when!" Grandma rolls her eyes looking for the right name. "Kantrovitzski—uh-uh, June, no? Her poor mother, *alavah sholem*, didn't like that, you can be sure!"

"Didn't like what, Grandma?"

Joan's face is getting red. "That's none of your business."

Grandpa's amazed. "She changed her name?"

Grandma nods. "She changed her name."

Now Uncle Sam makes the argument louder. "*Onyouka*, shut up! That is not for you to repeat."

"I knew I was right!" Grandma smiles.

Joan Whoever interrupts with a huff. "No! You are wrong! It is Jeanette—Jeanette Kantrovitz." She grabs her coat. "These lessons are over and I am leaving. Sam, are you coming with me?"

My uncle waves her away.

"Why did you have to change your name? Did you do something bad?" I'm curiouser as Alice in Wonderland.

"I did it for—professional purposes, just like your father changed his. Not that you'd understand what that means, you little brat."

My uncle is arranging his cards in his hand. "Joan, keep your lace undies on. I'll drive you after I beat the pants off my brother."

"No, thank you! I can walk!" And with a big sweep of her huge plaid coat she opens the door and exits!

"I think the lesson is over." Aunt Elaine doesn't seem bothered.

My father agrees. "I think the lessons are over, period."

"Well, Aaron, Avrahom, Vroomie, Itzack, Irving—that's the end of the lessons! Now you will have to pay me in cash!"

"The hell, I will! No woman can treat my kid like that! Consider the debt paid in full."

"OK, OK. So we begin again." My uncle shuffles the cards and they mutter at each other about cheating and dealing the cards.

Grandpa gets up and puts on his coat. "*Onyouka*, it's time! Put on your coat. I'm leaving."

Grandma gets up and puts her head in the kitchen. "Thelma, thanks for having us for Sunday dinner. We always enjoy how you cook the brisket. Right, Apoukah?"

Grandpa stands behind Sam and watches his sons arrange a fan of cards. "We need a ride home."

"You can walk! It's only a short distance. The exercise is good for you." Sam doesn't even look up at his father.

"Aaron?" Grandma walks to the door and waits for an answer.

"I gotta help Thelma. Besides, I wanna hear Sorahlah play my favorite song for me." He starts to sing, "*Besame mucho*—huh, Thel—that's our song, right, kiddo?"

Grandma speaks to Aunt Elaine. "How will you get home, Elonka?"

"Don't worry, *Onyouka*. Hugo is picking me up after he gets home from the bakery."

"Yeah, he's a regular dough boy." Uncle Sam takes every opportunity to poke fun at Elaine's husband, who is now working night-shift at Hermann's Bakery.

Aunt Elaine ignores them, kisses her father and mother, who exit muttering words in Hungarian that I recognize as not too nice. She goes back into the kitchen. My stepmother throws a towel at me.

I am still wondering about Joan Kane's name change. "Aunt Elaine, what does for professional purposes mean?"

"Well, it's like saying she needed to shorten her name; she wanted to make it more acceptable."

Uncle Sam nods to this. "She has her reasons just like your father."

My father answers him back. "Yeah, she doesn't want anybody to know she's Jewish. But I think she's queer besides."

"You're such a troublemaker. Shut up and *play* cards!" His brother is irked.

I am still confused. "But why is being Jewish a problem? This is America. There is no Holocaust here."

Thelma puffs on a cigarette. "Take our word for it. Sometimes it pays to soft pedal who you are—I mean your identity. Or change your nose!" Thelma laughs.

"Schmuel, did Joan have her nose fixed?" My aunt is shocked. I am Miss Echo. "She changed her nose?"

"GIN!" Uncle Sam slams the cards down on the table.

"What! You cheated. You had to cheat!" Daddy argues and angrily marks down the points, breaking the pencil in half. My father is hopping mad and deals the cards out sputtering at the same time. "Shirley, play our song. *Now!* We all know who's the cheater around here! Do you hear me? Move it! Play my song!"

Sam smacks down the cards just as he picks them up. "I knock with six points!"

My father, red as a beet, counts the cards. "You're full of crap! You haven't got the right number of cards. I didn't even get to draw."

Uncle Sam sneers. "So, I made a mistake! Big deal. Avramski, we're starting fresh!"

Daddy does a super fast shuffle with the cards, which go flying all over the floor.

Then he yells at me. "Get in here and play what I want to hear and do it now."

I drop the towel and rush to the piano. I play a pop version of "Besame Mucho." My father starts to sing louder than thunder while picking up the cards. Suddenly I rip into my Bach piece faster than Bach ever played it with absolutely no mistakes.

Uncle Sam's mouth drops in amazement. Daddy keeps on singing. Aunt Elaine serves the apple pie real quick and gives me a pleading look. Thelma walks in and out doing a crossword puzzle, puffs furiously on a cigarette, and pours out coffee for my father.

Before you know it, smooth as pudding, I go right back into my father's song and finish without missing a beat. Uncle Sam winks at me and shuffles the cards.

My father digs into the apple pie.

I earned my dessert!

Chapter Nineteen

AN ARTISTIC CONFIRMATION
1947 TO 1949

It's Sunday! Milton Wolf and I are hurrying up Beacon Street heading for the Confirmation rehearsal. It seems to me we practice too long and too much. I have so many other things that I want to do.

"I hope Mr. Schaffer and the rabbi don't keep us long. I can't be late for my extra piano lesson especially since today Miss Welker is making me practice for the audition." I'm talking to myself as well as Milton.

Milton gets annoyed. "I don't mind covering up about the extra piano lessons when your parents think you're at Confirmation practice, but what's this about an audition?"

"For a scholarship. Since they moved to Detroit and her baby Deanna Joy came, Aunt Elaine can't spare any money. And Uncle Sam says it's up to my father to pay for my lessons for a change. I've just got to get that scholarship or I'll die."

Miltie protests, "But my mother expects me home the same time as usual. How come your father swallows four-hour rehearsals on a Sunday? I think they should've figured it out by now."

"You exaggerate, Milton. My father doesn't care as long as he isn't schlepping me. You are a perfect angel, covering for me. The audition isn't for two weeks. We'll know what to tell your mother by then."

"It better be good. But what if your father won't let you accept it?"

"I will be able to arrange it. I just know, no matter what." Then I add, "Hey, maybe tell them you are coaching the girls in Hebrew like you did before your Bar Mitzvah. You could be an assistant again."

"My father will know for sure that I'm no rabbi's assistant, not at this *shul.*

We'll get caught. The rabbi could let it slip or something. Then it *will* be good-bye piano lessons."

"They can't know anything about these lessons, Milton. Promise me."

Milton would be even more surprised if he knew about the voice lessons I am getting as well. Since I began planning to sing for Confirmation, I have been taking a voice lesson at PCW on the Saturdays when I have no piano or composition. Miss Welker somehow got Mrs. Keister to pay for the lessons out of a special fund. I have said nothing to anyone—not even Miltie.

"Promise me!" I repeat and stop and wait for his answer.

"Yeah, yeah, I understand. I'll stick by you, Sor. We're best friends, aren't we?"

"I'm very nervous about it."

"About having a boy for a best friend?"

"No, silly, about the audition. I've never done a scholarship audition before!"

"You play the piano for people all the time. And you are going to sing today for the rabbi, aren't you?"

"Yes, but it's not the same."

We are climbing the steps to the synagogue doors. Milton grabs the heavy door and holds it for me. "C'mon, Shirley. The rabbi is waiting."

Just then, I spot another friend from high school and from the Confirmation group hurrying across the street. It's Leona Podolsky. "Go ahead, Miltie. I'll wait for Leona." Miltie shrugs and goes into the synagogue.

Leona is becoming a good friend. She likes to sing and is in Miss Steiner's special "A" choir. She and Doreen Halpern both take lessons from Miss Olean. But Leona is not into bragging about what she can do. Leona listens to me practice my song for Confirmation and gives me suggestions. She is also working with me on the Confirmation

Journal. Sometimes when we have an after school rehearsal, we walk up Shady Avenue on the way to the synagogue. Since we go right past her house, we can stop and get a drink until it's time to get to the rehearsal. That special time gives me a chance to confide in her about some of my problems with my stepmother. Leona is on my side—sympathetic, and we both share secrets.

One day, on the way to an after school Journal meeting, we stop at her house, get a drink, and just fool around experimenting with makeup. Her parents are out and she gets very mysterious and whispery. "Want to try out something with me?"

"Try out what?" I am always interested in what Leona proposes. She gets a lot of ideas from her older sister, Selma, about boys and stuff and fills me in on what I don't know. For me that's great since I never get any information from my family.

"You know, uh, like…" and then she rummages in her dresser drawer and comes up with a pack of Camels. She pops out a cigarette and pulls me into the bathroom. She closes the door and opens the window. Then she strikes a match and instantly puffs in and out, sending a long stream of smoke out the window. This smoking in the bathroom's too much like the experience when I burned the bathroom curtains and Grandma had to rescue me. But on the other hand, Eva does it, Uncle Sam does it, and now, Leona. So, what's the harm? She hands me the butt.

I gingerly take the glowing cigarette between my thumb and forefinger and inhale just like Humphrey Bogart does it in the movies. Suddenly my eyes are bugging out. I start to choke, cough, and spit into the sink. My stomach sucks in. My head is swimming. Tears stream down my face. Leona hands me a towel. "Wipe your eyes. You did a deep inhale. That's a lot for a first time!" I blow my nose in toilet paper. My throat feels like it is on fire.

"That's terrible," I finally manage to sputter. "Why do something that makes you feel so sick?"

Leona starts to laugh. "You just have to get used to it."

I admire Leona, who has a lot of what my grandma calls *chutzpah*. But I have no desire to go through that experience again. She hugs me and we are better friends than ever.

Now she takes the steps up to the synagogue doors two at a time, and we enter the dark hall and make our way down the aisle. The rabbi is standing there talking to the pianist. Milton is sitting slouched in the third row of seats. Leona sits down next to him.

The rabbi turns and catches sight of me. "You are late, Shirley. Give the accompanist the music. I want to hear how you sound before we put you on the program. What is the name of your piece?"

I have hardly put my coat down or taken a breath and I have to sing? Oh, well. I want to do this with Grandpa and Grandma there to hear me. "Uh, it's 'Shiru,' uh, 'Shiru L'ado Shem, Sing to the Lord.'" I give the music to the accompanist and walk up to the *bima*. I start to sing but realize the accompanist is playing the introduction. "Oops, sorry. Can we start again?" My stomach has those usual butterflies I get when doing something new. I'm usually the accompanist; now I'm on the other side of the piano! We begin again. This time only a crack and a squeak come out. The rabbi's eyes pop wide open.

"Shirley, are you sure you want to do this? The synagogue will be filled with people. You need to be thoroughly prepared." The rest of the Confirmation class is now filing in and taking seats.

I will do this! I will, I say to myself.

"I'm sorry, Rabbi Rose. I swallowed wrong. Begin again, please." Leona gives me an encouraging smile. Milton sits up straighter and directs his no nonsense look at me. I nod to the woman at the piano. This time I am sure of myself. My voice is high and clear. Milton and Leona applaud loudly. The other kids are googleeyed at how my voice sounds. I hear Patty Goldberg's voice shout, "Bravo!"

The rabbi's face lights up. "My goodness, Sorahlah, your voice is lovely. My wife told me you could sing, but not like that! Why aren't you singing with Cantor Adelsheim's choir anymore?"

"My grandfather says that…well…it's a long story, Rabbi. I'll tell you sometime." And he drops the subject since the rest of the class is waiting for rehearsal to begin.

Rabbi Rose reassures me. "Well, you certainly can sing this solo for Confirmation exercises. No problem."

Milton and Leona are grinning from ear to ear. I notice that the whole class is impressed. "Oh, thank you, thank you, Rabbi."

"But leave your music for the week so the accompanist can learn it."

"How will I practice without the music?" I get panicky.

"I'll look for your father at the men's club meeting and give it back to him."

"Uhhhhh—never mind, Rabbi, I just remembered I have another copy at home. She can have it!"

"Good! You should always have two copies of everything. You never know when it will come in handy. Make sure you have the voice part correctly and from memory."

"My uncle Willie who's a cantor is helping me with it."

Uncle Willie Hofstadter, who is not really my uncle but a distant relative on my grandmother's side, now sings at the Shaare Torah Synagogue on Murray Avenue. Grandma asks him to help me sing but not to say anything to Grandpa. Willie does not care about women singing with the men. "I tink vomen add someting very special to de service. I vill come to your house vun afternoon to practice and gif you a free voice lesson since you now haf a piano."

I remember thinking: *Hmmm, I guess an extra voice lesson wouldn't hurt me. It's nice he wants to do this for me. I'll need to make sure Thelma will not be there. They still do not think much of Willie after the salt incident.*

The rabbi wants to tell the whole world about my singing and coming performance. "I'm going to tell your father how pleased I am."

"Oh, Rabbi, no. He doesn't even know I'm singing for the Confirmation."

"Your parents don't know?"

"Uh! It's a special surprise. For their anniversary! Please don't say anything."

"A very wonderful and generous thing to do." The rabbi smiles at me.

"And you, Milton, are you planning some surprise as well? You always come early with Shirley and walk home with her."

"Uh, uh…no sir…Rabbi. I just make sure that Sor gets home OK since we practice so long—uh, late. Besides, uh—I am helping some other girls with their Hebrew. I enjoy being sorta like—a teacher—uh, an assistant."

The rabbi laughs. "But that sounds like a good idea. I'll speak to your father. Practice, Shirley. We don't have that many rehearsals left before June."

I better call Willie tonight and ask him to bring me another copy of the song.

ᴄᴏ

The rehearsal is a piece of cake. Afterwards, I hug Leona and Patty, who know what I'm up to, and head out the big doors. Miltie and I run down Shady Avenue past Wilkins. We cut through the fancy properties, past lots of driveways with chauffeurs polishing cars and ladies walking snow-white poodles and Great Danes and even a fluffy looking Persian cat. The gardens are full of bushes heavy with pink and purple and white spring flowers that smell like perfume. The trees droop with budding leaves and birds sing and flutter from branch to branch. It is a private road, and only an occasional car or truck passes through slowly—hardly moving. It's as quiet as the library reading room. No one seems to mind that we are what Milton warns is trespassing.

"I guess they are used to the students who study at Pennsylvania College for Women and all the young kids who attend classes there in the summer. We just probably look like two of the many who invade their quiet and their privacy all the time." I try to sound like I know the answers!

This particular day on Woodland Road walking and inhaling the fresh green around me and thinking about music and learning fills me with a longing inside that I want to last forever. I smile at Milton jumping over a pile of dirt some gardeners are spreading on the ground. Then, the smell hits me. "Yuck, Milton, now you will have manure on your shoes."

"Hey, kid! This is private property. Keep off." A man in overalls with white hair sticking out from under a railroad cap shoos us away.

Inside the music building, I stop and read the notices on the board. Milton is scraping his shoes off on the concrete outside the building.

He follows me inside. "What're you reading all those pages for?"

"That's how I know about the scholarship auditions Miss Welker's preparing me for. You can see all the recitals listed and news about students and performances everywhere."

"Yeah, but you can't go. So what's to read?"

"How can you find out about things if you aren't curious? Besides, maybe sometime I will get to go. Like, look! There's another notice on a big poster: *Opera Workshop coming this summer!*" *I need to find out about that. Hmmm! Who knows?* I think to myself. *But first things first.*

Miss Welker opens the door and I go in to take my lesson. Milton decides to wait for me in the lobby. I'm really glad he came with me today. It's getting late, and he always makes me feel safe when we walk home together. Milton is a great friend.

∽

It's Saturday morning and I am on my way back from my lessons. It has been a circus trying to keep up with my studies at school, practicing the piano, completing the assignments in composition, and now, taking a voice lesson every other week. My parents know about the piano lessons but don't make an issue of it after Uncle Sam lectures them. "She's getting lessons for free!" They do not know about the extras. They don't know I'm getting ready for a scholarship audition either even though I mentioned it at my final lesson with Joan Kane

The voice lessons are mostly just singing songs, which doesn't sound anything like what Doreen Halpern does. Renee tells me every chance she gets about her lessons. "I study with Miss Olean. " *She says her name like she's some kinda movie star.* "We do scales and exercises and Italian art songs. She is a real technical singing teacher and expects me to practice every day. Miss Steiner thinks Miss Olean is the best and wants all her 'A' choir sopranos to take lessons from her."

She talks an awful lot about how great it is to be in the top choir. But I do love watching and listening to her practice. She sings scales up and down just like what I do on the piano, but she does it with her voice, which is wonderful and high and sounds like a bell. *Nothing like mine! When I sing along with the opera on the radio, I can match the fast runs and fancy trills right along with the singers. Men and women! But I never sound good as Doreen.*

Doreen's mother tells Thelma, "Shirley should be studying with Miss Olean, too." Thelma just nods and then changes the subject. Of course, I do not let Renee know about all my extra lessons since Mrs. Halpern and Thelma buzz each other back and forth all the time.

I ask Miss Welker, "How can I get my voice to sound like my friend's?"

She explains, "Every voice is different, but you need to sound like yourself." Then she pauses and looks through a calendar on her desk. "There is a very famous singer, Birgit Nilsson, who is performing with the Pittsburgh Symphony next Sunday afternoon at Syria Mosque. I would like to take you to that concert. Then you will really hear a unique voice. Ask your parents if I might take you to the concert as my guest. In the meantime, I suggest you tell your voice teacher that you would like to sing something in Italian."

When I ask Mr. Akmajian, my voice teacher, about Italian art songs and exercises like my girlfriend, Renee, is doing, he just yawns and rolls his eyes. Then he tells me to buy a book of folk songs. "You have enough going on, kid." He adds, "All you have to do is take a bigger breath and let your voice just happen. That's all there is to it!" I don't let him know I can't buy a new music book. But amazingly, my father lets me go to the concert with Miss Welker after Thelma chides him. "It's free. Why not?"

Sunday comes. I put on my best dress and meet Miss Welker at the top of Forbes Street. We ride the streetcar into Oakland and get off right by the big building she tells me is the University of Pittsburgh. I practically strain my neck looking up at the high building, which looks like a pencil standing on its end. Miss Welker hurries me along past Fifth Avenue to where Syria Mosque, the concert hall, sits. *Amazing! It has big metal doors that remind me of my first trip to the library.* There is a man in a fancy outfit and hat holding the door for people—all dressed up and streaming into a big hall with high ceilings. The ticket takers are dressed in black. The ushers who show us to our seats wear black skirts or pants, white shirts, and black ribbon ties around their necks. We have two seats right on the end of the row halfway up the middle section. "Sit on the aisle, Shirley. You will see better." Miss Welker hands me a program. The stage has chairs and music stands, and men and women are filing in with violins, trumpets, flutes, and every kind of instrument. They are getting their music out and tuning up their instruments. I can hardly believe my eyes. My ears start to crackle with the sounds of the horns, the percussion, and the strings.

Even though I've seen Miss Ziegler conduct the orchestra at Allderdice, the students take a long time getting quiet, and they make scratchy sounds. When the conductor of the Pittsburgh Symphony takes his place and bows to the audience, the feeling and the sounds are not the same. Everyone is immediately silent. I do not look at the program. My eyes are glued to the stage. Then he turns to the orchestra. He is wearing a long black coat with what looks like tails in the back. He quickly raises his arms and I can see his baton hesitate, and then the music begins. I feel as though I'm sitting right in the middle of the stage and my whole body is vibrating. I'm rigid, totally unable to move, and realize I'm practically holding my breath. My heart seems to beat in time with the conductor, and when the piece ends, I am devastated. I want the music to go on and on and on. The audience applauds loudly. He turns around and bows. His bow tie is pure white like his shirt.

"Did you enjoy the piece, Shirley? Mostly Wagner today." Miss Welker laughs when she sees that I'm frozen with my mouth open.

I panic inside myself. *Is it over? Where's the singer?*

Miss Welker seems to read my mind. "It is time for intermission now. Miss Nilsson is on the second half of this concert. Do you want to go into the lobby?" She's standing up. I am relieved that there's going to be more.

"No, thank you! I just want to look at the stage and read the program."

Miss Welker goes up the aisle, but I can't concentrate on the program. My mind doesn't want to let me think about reading. Wagner? It is a name I've heard on the opera broadcasts, but it doesn't really have meaning for me. I *will* have to look him up in the library at school now that I know he is a composer.

Intermission ends. Everyone takes their seats. The lights dim, and then suddenly thunderous applause begins as a woman in a lovely flowing gown comes on stage. *Good heavens! She is a big woman and not very young. Is this the singer?* She speaks to the audience in a very strong and loud voice, mentioning the songs she will sing and telling a story about each number. She nods to the conductor, lowers her head, and raises it quickly. Then the orchestra begins and the sound of her voice fills the big hall. "She's singing a Brahms song in German." Miss Welker points to the title in the program. My eyes are almost a blur of tears. *To hear this voice makes me aware, and I understand that there certainly is a difference in voices! If Doreen wants to take a lesson in how to sing, she should listen to Birgit Nilsson.* Being there in the concert hall is not the same as listening to somebody on the radio! It's alive and overwhelming. She sings several other songs—Lieder, Miss Welker calls them. I applaud along with everyone else. When she leaves the stage, I want to run after her. "She will do an encore, don't worry." My piano teacher really knows the whole routine.

And out comes this glorious singer again. Only, wow! She has on a white Dutch cap, a brightly embroidered dirndl skirt, a matching white off-the-shoulder blouse and wooden shoes. Everyone laughs and the clapping hands are like windmills. She speaks. "I will sing 'Vergebliches standchen' by Brahms."

Miss Welker whispers, "It's a German art song."

The singer explains the German for the audience. "This is about a boy who wants to visit a girl. Her mother has warned her not to let him in the house when she is not at home and…" She finishes telling the story. I laugh to myself. *Well, that certainly sounds familiar to me.* The conductor raises his baton, and I lean on the edge of my seat. *Look at her hands on her hips; she is doing a wooden shoe kind of heel-toe bang-bang dance as the orchestra plays. How she sings! She makes the story so clear; her face is shining. I want to learn that song.* I turn to my piano teacher and shout over the loud applause, "I want to learn that song!" She nods.

On the ride home Miss Welker and I talk about the music and the singer and what it means to perform on stage. "How can I thank you, Miss Welker? There is nothing in my life that can beat this day! I don't want it to be over. Where can I get that song?"

"You will have many more opportunities for concerts and perhaps even seeing an opera on the same stage. Now you can hear how voices change and grow, and yours will, too. And if you want to have that song, you will need to get a copy of the Brahms book, which is in German. But you can start first with an English translation. You know, there are copies of all the Lieder in the Carnegie Music Library. They have recordings you can listen to and check out."

I am embarrassed to tell my teacher that we do not have a phonograph. Only my Uncle Sam has recordings he keeps locked up in his fur store. I never noticed if he has a phonograph. *I'll have to figure out how to get one for myself. Now the library will be a place for me to learn to read music and words in another language just like I first learned to read the word* sandwich. It suddenly seems such a long time ago.

That night at home during dinner, I speak about my experience. My sister thinks it's great. Thelma doesn't say anything. My father makes me play "Besame Mucho" four times. The last time he dances around the living room with my stepmother wearing her apron with a dishtowel over her shoulder.

"Next song I want you to learn, Shirley Ruth, is "It Had to Be You." See if you can find it on the radio. Or get that piano teacher to take you to a concert with real singers like Frank Sinatra or Rosemary what's-her-name."

♋

For the next several weeks, I begin reading the want ads and thinking about getting a part-time job to pay for a phonograph— used, of course—and spare money to get some singing books. My father does not let me do baby-sitting in the neighborhood, and I never get any allowance for taking care of the house or my sister. Then on a Saturday coming home from my piano lesson, I walk down Forbes Street to buy a skyscraper ice cream cone at Isaly's with my saved-up milk money. I'm walking and licking my toasted almond fudge when I spot a sign right next to the Squirrel Hill Newsstand. *Wanted! Part-time Accompanist—Apply upstairs. Experience helpful.* Upstairs? Where? There is a glass entry door with steps behind it right next to the newsstand. I look at the print on the door: *Kelly Studio of Dance.* I quickly finish my cone, wipe my mouth off with a paper napkin, and take the stairs up.

I can hear a piano—a clackity one—and pounding that is deafening. When I push the door open, there are dozens of little girls and a few boys making their feet go a mile a minute. They have on shoes with metal tips making their feet clap out a loud rhythm. This must be the tap studio Miss Long at Allderdice talked about in class one day: "If you want to learn to tap so you can be a Broadway baby." I didn't pay too much attention when she said it. But here right in front of my nose—which I'm learning to follow a lot—is a real job opportunity.

A thin, dark-haired woman dismisses the children, who gather up their bags and regular shoes and hurry out the door with their mothers or baby-sitters.

"Are you here for the next class?" The woman is speaking to me.

"No, I'm here to be your accompanist!"

"My goodness! What luck! You can start in fifteen minutes with the next class. My name is Miss Kelly. And you are? Never mind. Sit down and warm up your fingers."

I immediately sit down and run the C scale, which I know very well by now. I look through the music on the piano. Miss Kelly is watching me carefully. "Oops! I'm not a great sight reader," I tell her as she welcomes the next class, "but I can play anything you want off the top of my head."

And that's what I do. Miss Kelly gives the class what she calls a combination and then I put music to it. My fingers make the piano tap right along with their shoes. The hour flies by and I catch on to the whole routine like the devil.

She smiles a big smile at me. "You have a job! Leave your name, Social Security number, address, and phone number on this sheet. You will get minimum wage. Come back Monday at four p.m. I look forward to having you play for my classes." Then she puts on the phonograph with some jazz music for an advanced class.

I don't even know what minimum wage means. And I have no idea what my Social Security number is. I figure I will ask Grandma before Monday. By the time I get home, Thelma is angry since I did not get the salad cut on time or set the table. My lateness is not usual for me, and Barbara had to wait on the porch since I forgot to put the key under the doormat. I'm going to need to be better organized to keep my secret activities in order.

For five weeks I manage to get to the dance studio every Monday and on Saturday after my lessons. Being the dance accompanist for Miss Kelly goes way beyond tapping and is way different than playing for modern dance class at Allderdice. I begin to learn ballet positions, stretching exercises, and some jazzy moves. Excitedly, I start writing notes on music paper to create a book for Miss Kelly. She is thrilled and encourages me to jump right in and create all I want to. All this activity makes me barely get home on time, but my stepmother and father are working late. They don't notice I'm late, too. My sister Barbie helps me get things ready so I don't get yelled at.

Miss Kelly, however, keeps after me for the full information on the paper. "Shirley! Your Social Security number! I need it in order to pay you."

"Yeah, I know. Sorry, Miss Kelly. I keep forgetting. Uh, can't you just pay me in cash? My father does that with his customers so there's no tax."

"This is a matter of business. And business is business!" She is very definite about that.

After dinner that night, the phone rings and my father answers it. "Hello. Who? Miss what? Kelly. So. Uh, huh. Yes. Oh, I see. She did, huh? Well, guess what? My kid, my daughter's not working for any dance studio. She's underage and she can't take a job without my permission. Hmmm, uh, huh. Yeah! I don't care how talented she is. Really? Just send the money you owe her in a check. No, she can't come back anymore." And with that he bangs down the receiver and turns on me with a scowl. "I ought to beat you black and blue deciding to do some jerky thing like playing piano in a queer place."

"But it's a studio with little kids learning to tap dance. Daddy, please. I need to have extra money to buy a phonograph and new music books!"

"That's what I get for letting you take lessons and go to free concerts. You must think money grows on trees."

With that he reaches for the fur whip, cracks it in the air, and makes me open my hands palms up. But as he aims, I turn and bolt up the steps and lock myself in the bathroom. Then I hear footsteps and a knock on the door.

"Shirley, I have to use the bathroom." It's my stepmother. "You should know by now what is going to set your father off. You should not do something without permission. Just go to bed. He'll forget about it by tomorrow."

How will I ever face Miss Long, who thinks it's great that I have a job playing for the Kelly dance family? My friend Patty tells me, "Be happy your father did not cancel your piano lessons. Besides, Confirmation is coming soon and you will need to work on your speech as well as your song. At least you know you can always get a job there when you are in charge of your own life."

Fat chance they'll hold the job open that long! As it turns out, I run into Miss Kelly on Forbes Avenue one day, and she's glad to see me and says she understands my predicament. Then she takes twenty dollars out of her purse and hands it to me. "That's about what you had coming for your accompanying."

"But you don't have my Security number."

"Don't concern yourself. Keep playing and studying. You are a great accompanist. Anytime you want to pop in to run a tap number through for me, just come up the stairs."

I never do go up the stairs again. But I hide the twenty dollars to put towards a phonograph player and maybe even the Brahms book at Wagner-Bund's music store on Liberty Avenue downtown.

Chapter Twenty

PERMANENT DAMAGES
MAY 1949

Thelma is throwing the breakfast dishes and garbage into the sink. A cigarette is hanging from her mouth. I am hysterical and crying.

"Oh, stop your sniveling! You look fine. It's what your father wants. He is very particular about how his girls look. Wipe the snot off your face!"

I frantically try to pull my new dress down over my knees. "I look like a stupid clunk. And my hair...my hair is ruined...ruined forever!" I catch a look at myself in the mirror over the dining room buffet. My hair's a pile of frizzy curls, bushy bangs and shorter than ever before. The dress barely makes it across my newly blooming chest. I grab a dishtowel to wipe my face.

My stepmother, agitated as usual, is getting ready to go downtown to my father's jewelry store. "Where's my crossword—oh, there! I need something to keep me busy on the bus ride and at the store. I'm bored crazy down there. Don't forget, Shirley! Set the table, turn on the soup, and cut a salad. Leave out the green peppers; your father gets too gassy! Oh, and hang up the dresses your father got for you yesterday. They cost a pretty penny, you know. Take care of your clothes. You should appreciate that he wants you to look up-to-date for your Confirmation. And that new permanent wave is better than those stupid plaits you used to have and the way you let your hair hang. Just think! You won't have to try to curl it; it's all curly by itself." She puts on her long leather gloves, sets the veil of her feathered hat across her face, and checks her lipstick in the mirror over the mantel. Her tongue flicks a smear of lipstick off her two front teeth that have a large space between them. She spits a thread of tobacco off her lips as she shoves a new pack of cigarettes into her purse, pulls open the front door, and hurries down the steps and up the hill to catch the bus.

In a minute the phone is in my hand and I dial my grandma. She hears my sobbing breathy voice. "*Gevalt*, Sorahlah? *Vos iz, mit dir?* What's wrong? Sorahlah, Sorahlah...my *shaynical.* Stop your crying! *Genug mit geshreeyan.*"

"They chopped it off." I cry even louder.

"Did someone hurt you? Answer me. *Sorahlah! Genug iz genug!* Enough! Stop it this instant!!"

"They cut it off! All of it off—chopped it..."

"Yoy-oy-yoy! What did they cut? Are you bleeding?"

"If you could see my hair—it's gone. I don't look like your Sorahlah. I don't look like anyone's Sorahlah. I'm a horrible mess. And Sunday is the big audition and look at me. Just look. No one'll even want to listen to such a mess."

Grandma's trying to soothe my hysterical sobbing. "How did this all happen? Where is your hair?"

I speak through my tears. "On the floor of the beauty shop. Chopped off. They hooked me up to this horrible machine with wires and put some stinky stuff on my hair, and look at me. Ugly! Ugly! Ugly! And the dress. My father insisted Thelma buy me this dress for the Confirmation—and six more—one more ugly than the next one."

Grandma is full of disbelief. "*Gott in himmel!* They still use those electric chair—I mean—hair machines?"

"My hair! My hair! They just chopped off my hair and bought me ugly clothes, and I'm nothing but a big frizz ball with ugly breasts and hairy legs and..."

"You have other clothes. Just wear another one."

"He took them in the car to give them away to some poor children. And I have six other new ones just like this; they don't fit, and I need a bra and stockings and regular high heels like the other girls are going to wear. Ugly! I hate myself!"

"*Oy! Veyes mir!* Sounds just like your Aunt Elaine."

I blow my nose in the dishtowel. "What? Who?"

"Your Aunt Elaine and your mother, *alavah sholem.* The two of them—same thing—only they brought it on themselves."

"What do you mean? What are you talking about?"

"Before you were born, your mother was feeling big and fat with you in her stomach, and your Aunt Elaine wanted to make her glamorous. So the two of them walked into a beauty shop and got the whole *megillah*! Dyed! Permed! Talk about frizzy! *Ich chab gezacht to deina mama und meina tochter, 'Gornisht helfin!'* I was so mad at both of them…they vas like you say—real frizz balls. Nothing could help. *Deine tatah*—Your father had a fit!"

I grow calmer and thoughtful. "So why's he do it to me now? And how can I go to my audition—" I catch myself. "I mean, Confirmation rehearsal looking like this? I'm a mess!"

"Do what I tell you. Go to the shower and wash your hair three times with some shampoo. Then rinse it out two times with water with lemon squeezed in and then again with some vinegar. And wash and rinse *alles*—all of it over again. But be careful of *deina eigen*. Do not get it in your eyes."

"My eyes?"

"It will burn your eyes. Keep them covered with a washrag. And bring the dress to me. I will make it fit. Now listen and *macht was ist chab ge rett tsu dir. Fer shtayf?* You understand? Your mama has vinegar under the sink and I know there is lemon in the ice box."

"Thank you, Grandma. I will do what you ask of me. I understand." Then I pause. "Grandma…"

"Yes, *meine kleinecal.*"

"Did you call my bubbie to invite her to my Confirmation?"

"She and your aunt Mayme and Uncle Louis are coming and will bring your cousins."

"Oh, thank you, Grandma, thank you. Daddy wouldn't do it."

"I know. *Mein zohn bist a nahr,* sometimes. Now go and shampoo."

"Are you and Grandpa coming? I have a surprise for you."

"Of course. What is the surprise?"

"You'll see. You and Grandpa will be very proud, I hope."

"Go shampoo and bring the dress to me. Do it now!"

"Yes, Grandma. Oh, and Grandma, don't speak about the audition, please."

"I know all about it, Sorahlah. Milton's mother called and we discussed it. I say nothing—*gornicht.* But, go, do what I say."

"Oh, my. I almost forgot! I have to wait. Willie Hofstadter is coming to make sure I know the 'Shiru' song."

"It will still be a surprise for me to hear my *kleinecal's*—my little one's beautiful voice. But, please call him Uncle Willie. He's a distant cousin but a religious and observant man as well as the cantor of Shaare Torah. It is more respectful of his place in the Jewish community. He is the one who found the song for you and wants to help you. Shower afterwards and come to me...and no more tears! Promise."

"Thank you, Grandma. I will bring the dress for you to fix later today."

Grandma speaks softly to me on the phone. "You will not be ugly! You will be *shayne wie goldt*—gorgeous! *Zei gezunt*...be well."

Then the doorbell rings. "Oh, Grandma, I can see. He's here already. I need to hang up."

❧

I go to the door and let Uncle Willie in. He hugs me awful tight and I have to pull away from him.

"Sorahlah, my dear child, you look vonderful. But your hair is different. Vhat did you do to it? And your dress? You are really growing up...fast!"

I go to the piano and put the lid covering the keys, up. "I need to practice quickly, Uncle Willie. I have to take a..."

"Please, just Villie. I am *not* your uncle. I am your father's distant cousin."

He goes to the piano and takes music out of a worn leather envelope under his arm. "Here is the extra copy I made by hant for you after you called me."

"The accompanist has my only copy. Thank you for doing another one for me."

Willie pinches my cheek. "Anything for my little Sorahlah, who is not so little anymore. Yes? Come! I play and you vill sit next to me and sing in your beautiful voice. Yes?"

"OK." I sit next to him and wait for him to play the introduction. He moves closer to me and starts to play, and then as I start to sing, he throws his head back singing loudly along with me.

"Uncle Willie—uh—Willie!" I can hardly hear myself singing. "Could you just play for me?"

He puts his arm around my shoulder and slides closer. I suddenly want this practicing to be over very quickly.

"You need, dear child, to learn to breathe correctly. You breathe too high. You need to breathe here below vhere your legs join." Suddenly his one hand is pressing my stomach and moving down while he presses my shoulder with his other hand. "The lower you feel de brett in your body deh…" I jump up as he grabs my waist. Then I struggle away from the bench and fall to the floor but quickly pick myself up.

"Sorahlah, singing is a very physical ting. Do not be so resisting."

"Please, just play the music for me and I will sing." I place myself behind him and off to the side almost into the dining room. He then plays louder and sings along at the top of his voice. I just go through the music and make no comment. When the piece is over, he wants to give me a voice lesson.

"Not today, Uncle Willie. I need to get ready to take a show… uh—my grandma is coming over soon to help me fix my dress and hair. I expect her any minute."

"Oh! Not Uncle Villie, sveetheart, just call me Villie. Inconvenient for lesson today. Anoder time den, my beautiful singer. Vee vill have some special time togeder. Yes?" He grabs me and tries to plant a wet kiss on my face. It lands on my ear as I turn away. His black moustache scrapes my cheek. My hands shove him away and I rush to open the door for him. "Such a grown up young lady, yes?" He almost falls out the door as I bang it shut. I put on the safety chain and double lock the door. I kick his leather envelope under the piano bench.

My body starts to shake and the beginning of tears lie behind my eyes. *No! Grandma is right. Genug mit geshreeyan—enough screaming and tears for one day.* I rummage under the sink and open the icebox. My trembling hands hold the lemon and vinegar. I wash and rinse my hair over the sink three times. *Oy! I didn't take off my clothes and I forgot to shampoo first!* I practically rip off the wet clothes and leave them in a soaking heap on the cold tile floor. Under the hot shower, I shampoo my hair three times and then I scrub my body with my father's Lifebuoy soap. Thoroughly!

Chapter Twenty-one

FOR PROFESSIONAL PURPOSES
MAY AND JUNE 1949

"Very fine, Shirley. You have improved a lot. You need to stay calm." Miss Welker, my piano teacher is trying to get me to relax.

"But, Miss Welker, I'm so nervous. This is a very important audition. I will not be able to continue if..."

"Don't worry. I have spoken to Mrs. Keister, who gives most of the money for the scholarships. She understands the situation."

"What if I make a mistake?"

"Everyone makes a mistake during an audition." She gives me a hug.

"Miss Welker, the sign says, *Auditions in Piano, Voice, Other Instruments*. Does that mean there's a scholarship for singing?"

"Yes, there is."

"Is one person allowed to do more than one audition? I mean, could I sing, too?"

"I didn't know you would want to sing for a scholarship today, and I already have you scheduled to audition only for piano lessons. How many things can you do today?"

"I was just wondering if I could continue taking the voice lessons on the alternate Saturdays?"

"Well, I don't know if..." She looks at my face and then suddenly she exclaims, "Why not! Do you know an appropriate song?"

"Appropriate? Uhhh—I know 'Shiru.' It's a Hebrew song for my Confirmation."

"I don't think that is a good idea for this particular group of people, uh, auditioners. Don't you know another piece? Something from your voice lessons?"

Mr. Akmajian has cancelled the lessons for several weeks while he was out of the country. I don't want to say anything. "I know 'Besame Mucho' and, ooh, 'The Star-Spangled Banner'—I know 'The Star-Spangled Banner' completely by heart. But—I don't have the music."

"'Besame Mucho'? Did your voice teacher give you that?"

I shake my head. "It's a pop piece off the radio…"

"No! Never mind! 'The Star-Spangled Banner' will be fine. Just tell them you will do one song—by, mmmm—just say, a capella." And then she spells it out for me: "a-c-a-p-e-l-l-a. Now go!"

"But, I'm so…"

"You will survive. Now do it!"

I go out into the hall where Miltie, my friend, is waiting for me. He is becoming very impatient. "What took you forever?"

I shush him and take a fresh application form from the table, chew on the end of a pencil, and begin writing very neatly.

"What're you doing now?"

"I have to fill out another form for the audition." A thought occurs to me. "Uh oh—I better fix my name up." I put down my Bach book, look at it, and then copy the name of the music company letter by letter on the form. "S-c-h-i-r-m-e-r. Good! That looks much better. Now for my first name. How about Sally? Yes….Sally Schirmer." I am muttering to myself as I write.

"Sor! What are you writing? Who is Skirmer?" Milton is looking over my shoulder.

"You pronounce it Shirmer, Miltie. The *c* is silent. It's <u>Schirmer</u> …S-A-L-L-Y—Sally Schirmer. It's me! It's my new name."

"Sally? Are you nuts? That's Irish!"

"So? What's wrong with that?"

"Why would you want to change your name anyway? Besides, with your dark eyes and hair and the noses in your family, no one will ever believe you're Irish."

"My grandfather has blue eyes and he used to have red hair. And Sally is a great name. You don't have to be Irish to have that name. But maybe…" I wet the eraser and rub out the first name. "There, what do you think of that?"

David reads aloud. "S-A-R-A? I don't understand why you can't use just plain Shirley."

"Milton! I haven't got time to discuss it now. It's something important I need to do."

"OK, OK! But if you are gonna use Sara, at least put an *h* on the end."

A tall girl whom I recognize as another of Miss Welker's students comes out of the audition room. A woman who's been standing at the door goes right over to her and hugs her. *Must be her mother.* I feel my nose start to itch.

"Thank you, Miss Carter. You will hear from the committee in about two weeks. Who's next?" It's the woman who seems to be in charge of auditions. I hand her the paper. "Uh, huh! Miss— Schirmer?" She holds the paper up to the light. "What is the first name? I can't quite make out the name with all the smeary streaks."

"Sara. Sara Schirmer."

"With an *h* on it." Milton adds his own spelling.

"Milton!" I roll my eyes at him.

"Are you playing or singing?" Her finger is running down a list of names. "I don't see your...?" She keeps trying to check for someone named Schirmer. *I hope I didn't spoil my chances by changing my name at the last minute.*

"Miss Welker said it was OK. I am doing both." I point to my own name on the list and smile weakly.

She just shrugs her shoulders and asks, "Do you want to sing or play your piece first? Is he your accompanist?" She points at Milton. I shake my head vigorously.

Milton is puzzled. "Sing? What do you mean sing?"

"I'll sing first, please."

I see how bewildered Milton is. "I'll explain later." I follow the lady into the room where there are three people seated at a table: a large woman in a flowered hat and two other people. There's a *big* what Miss Welker calls a concert grand in the room. They are all making notes on paper that looks like a copy of the list of names. My stomach has more than its usual fill of butterflies.

The flowered hat speaks. "I am Mrs. Keister. We need to get started." Her eyes go from me to the list to the form I filled out, and then back at me. "It says on your form that you are—" She stops! She checks the list again. My heart is beating very fast. "Hmm. I somehow thought your name was Shirley. I must have misunderstood. Is it Sarah?" I nod. "Well, go ahead and play…Sarah."

I go over to the keyboard and find a pitch and begin singing 'The Star-Spangled Banner' in my best high operatic voice. Mrs. Keister jumps out of her chair and interrupts me while she points with her pencil to the list of names.

"My goodness, child! I thought you were going to play the piano."

"I am, uh, next. But I really want to sing. I mean, I love playing, but is it all right if I sing for a scholarship, too? I mean Miss Welker said it would be all right to sing 'The Star-Spangled Banner' by Mister A. Capella…"

They all seem very amused. I don't know what's so funny at all.

"Go ahead and sing the piece, Miss? Schirmer? Sarah? Hmm." Mrs. Keister shakes her head totally bewildered.

I get my pitch from the piano again and repeat my operatic performance. I can see their eyes are all open wide especially when I take the last note in a very high full voice.

"Well, you certainly can sing, can't you?" Mrs. Keister is making lots of notes on my form in front of her. "Are you able to play the Bach?"

"Oh, yes, perfectly from memory." And I sit down and play the piece without waiting one minute for permission and without any mistakes. My hands are trembling. I am sure everyone sees the sweat running down from my hair. Mrs. Keister is smiling like a lit-up candle, and she starts to applaud and suddenly stops when the others look at her.

"Wait in the hall, miss…uh…your name? Sarah? Sarah Schirmer?" She is still smiling.

"Yes, m'am. Sarah with an *h*." When I go into the hall, Milton is waiting and looks like he is sweating, too.

"Gosh, it's hot in this building. Why is your face so red?"

"It's crazy but I am more nervous now than when I started. I just have to win those scholarships, Milton. I need to get enough money to pay for lessons in voice and piano. And Miss Welker thought it would be OK. She already helped me get free lessons in composition with Dr. Whitmer. And the voice lessons, too, and..."

"Dr. Whitmer? It sounds like you're gonna write a story about somebody who is sick!"

"Don't be smart, Milton Wolf. You know I'm trying to learn how to write down my own music on paper. That's what they call it when you take composer lessons—composition. He takes me right before my piano lesson so I don't have to make two trips here to PCW."

"Well, Sorahlah—'scuse me, Shirley—oops...what's the latest name...oh, yes...Sarah. When do you expect to squeeze in three lessons and do your regular school homework and get ready for Confirmation, and...?"

"Don't you worry about it, Milton! I'll manage whatever it takes."

Right at that minute the audition lady comes out and lets me know that I will hear in the mail about the scholarships in about two weeks.

"Let's get out of here before it gets dark." Milton grabs my arm and pulls me out the door. "My parents are gonna be fit to be tied because I'm so late." Then Milton sounds off at me. "Two weeks! I don't know if I can stand the pressure."

I follow him out of the music building and up Woodlawn Road. He is a great friend and always takes my side even though he seems mad at me for the moment.

ভ৹

Milton and I are on the front porch playing a good game of war. He's not too happy when I win again.

"You always win! Sorahlah, you are like a card shark."

"That's not true."

"Well, you must do something when you shuffle the deck. I've never seen anyone do it so fast."

"You've never seen my Uncle Sam. He flips those cards even faster. He taught me how."

Milton jumps up suddenly. "I hear somebody coming. I'll bet it's the mailman. Maybe you got your letter about the scholarship."

"Quick, Miltie, I need to catch him before Thelma, I mean, my mother gets the mail."

"Never mind, that's only David with his new wagon. Hey, Davie, how goes it?"

"Wagon?" I'm very curious.

"Yeah! He's delivering the *Pittsburgh Press*, now. That heavy canvas bag he had to schlep around made his back hurt so his father bought him a Flyer wagon."

I catch my breath. "It's a red wagon...a little red wagon."

"Nah, Sorahlah—it's a regular red wagon."

I am suddenly angry. "Don't argue. I know a little red wagon when I see one. And how many times do I have to tell you? Sarah. My name is Sarah!"

"What are you getting so steamed-up about?"

I turn my face away from him. *Why am I taking my feelings out on Milton?* "Oh, you know, girls sometimes...uh..."

"You sound like my mother!" He goes down to the sidewalk and talks to David. "So, David! How's business?"

I recover and smile at David who is in front of the house. "You must be doing very well with your little red wagon."

"This ain't no little wagon. It's regular size. Here, catch your *Press*."

He throws a folded paper at me, but Milton cuts in front of me like a football player and catches it.

I mutter under my breath. "I had a red wagon once. It would've fit in the back of the car. I know it would've!"

"Huh? Whadz you say?" Milton tosses the paper onto the glider on the porch. I do not answer him. He ignores me. "Hey, Davie, you got regular customers?"

"You bet! I got the whole street—from the bottom to the top of the hill. And I get tips, too."

I'm thinking about when I collected pop bottles for five cents. "I bet it's a lot easier to get the money when you have a red wagon."

"Not if you have to pull that wagon up the hills!" He continues rolling up the papers and throwing them right at the screen doors on every porch. He yells, "Bull's-eye," every time he hits the door.

Miltie goes back onto the porch and puts the cards neatly into the box.

"Hey, Sor—oops, sorry I mean, Shirley—ouch—Sarah with an *h*, I gotta get goin'; we have a dress rehearsal for Confirmation tonight. I'll meet you by the telly pole promptly at six-thirty p.m. Hey! There's the mailman! He's coming down the hill now."

I run down the porch steps and hit the sidewalk just as the mailman gets to the neighbor's house. He sees how excited I am.

"Hi, Shirley. I have a letter here, but I don't think it's the one you've been waiting for. It's addressed to a S-A-R-A-H S-C-H-I-R-?"

I grab the letter out of his hand and begin to open it. The mailman takes it back.

I try to take it out of his hand. "That's me! It's me." But he holds the letter high over his head where I can't reach it.

"Just a minute, now! I thought your name is Shirley Schiffman.

"It is, I mean— that's my old name. I have a new name."

"Why would you want to change your name? Teenage craze?"

I pause for a moment and then try to explain it to him. "Well—I had to do it—at least for now...for...for—" The mailman and Milton both have their eyes on my face. And then for the first time in my life, I speak deliberately with a new strong voice as I hold out my hand: *"For professional purposes."*

The End

EPILOGUE
JUNE 1949

When the letter about the Scholarship comes, I'm ecstatic! Mrs. Keister will pay for all the lessons at PCW.* I am careful, however, to hide the letter inside my English class notebook. I'll wait for the right time to tell everyone after the Confirmation exercises are over.

The Confirmation program takes place on a bright Sunday afternoon in June. The class lines up in the hallway behind the synagogue doors. We all have on white robes. The girls are carrying red roses; the boys wear boutonnières. As the doors open, I scan the crowd seated in the synagogue and spot my sister's head popping up and down looking for me. She's seated between Thelma and my father. But I don't see the rest of my family. Then the music for the processional starts.

We are all walking just as we rehearsed it. My head keeps craning to see Grandma and Grandpa. There's Uncle Sam! He winks at me. My sister waves her hand. No one else is visible. Oh, well, perhaps they are seated far to the side. We take our places on the *Bima*. All the speeches and songs we sing as a group go fine. But each time we stand up, the rabbi blocks my view. Then I spot Patty Goldberg's mother seated next to my cousin Willie. Unfortunately, I could not stop Grandma from inviting him. Even when I tried to tell her about my experience with the singing lesson, she shushed me and just shook her head. "He is a member of the religious community. Do not repeat that story again!" But she hugs me and says, "my *shaynical*…mine *zuise kind*…*oy, Gottes mir*…my dear sweet child!" I know she feels unable to do anything but remain silent.

When it's time to sing my solo 'Shiru L'ado Shem', I feel my insides turn over, but I take a deep breath, wait for the accompanist to play and begin singing. I know it doesn't sound as loud as when I practiced at home in the bathroom, but every note is correct. I can see my father's eyes are wide open and Thelma's jaw drops when I hit the last high note. Willie has a stiff smile on his face. Patty's mother is upright and starts to applaud immediately as soon as I finish. Dr. Canter, the Wolfs and others applaud. And there is Miss Welker, in the last row, smiling and nodding. The rabbi raises his hand for silence and says, "No applause, please! It is *Shevuot*; this *is* the synagogue, *you know*." I can tell some people are making comments to each other in spite of the rabbi's instructions. I can feel my face is red.

After the recessional, everyone is invited to a reception with punch and cookies. My parents make no comments about my singing. Uncle Sam is not in sight. Willie keeps approaching me and I manage to avoid him. My friends congratulate me, and a few of the members of the congregation tell me I have a lovely voice and want to know if I am taking lessons. I just nod. But where are my cousins or Bubbie or Aunt Mayme? And Grandma and Grandpa— where are they? Even Miss Welker has vanished.

Later in the afternoon, I find out that Willie let it slip that morning about my singing in the *Shul*. Grandpa became infuriated and refused the ride Willie offered him. He would not allow Grandma to go either. I never knew what happened to the rest of my mother's family. Even though I'm disappointed, I am resigned to the fact that some things will never change.

That evening, Dr. Canter is a guest for dinner. He says, "You did a nice job singing in Hebrew..." when the phone interrupts him. Thelma answers the extension on the desk next to the dinner table. "What, oh? Just a minute." She puts her hand over the receiver "It's some woman calling for a Mrs. Keister explaining about the forms for *Shirley's* scholarship that need to be signed." Thelma is drumming her fingers on the dining room table; Daddy begins to swear and shakes his head. "Scholarship? What? Uh, uh—no way. No kid of mine needs charity!" *So much for the right time to tell them!*

Thelma speaks to the voice on the phone, holding out the receiver so that my father and Dr. Canter hear it, too. "Look, Miss whoever you are, we are not interested in whatever it is you're offering." The voice continues. "We are sure you are so proud that Shirley has won a full scholarship to study music as a special student at PCW. We just need your signature on the forms that are coming in the mail so that we can process the award." My father pounds his fist on the table sending the silverware flying. Thelma doesn't hesitate one second as she rudely answers, "Our daughter Shirley does not need your scholarship. Give it to the next person in line." With that she bangs the receiver down.

I'm shaking with anger and embarrassment. My father and Thelma start questioning me about how this happened. By this time, I'm crying so hard my father threatens to give me something to really cry about. Dr. Canter tries to calm him down. But before my father can say another word, I'm up the stairs and locked in my bedroom. After dinner, I hear my father arguing at the top of his voice with Dr. Canter and then with Uncle Sam on the phone about the whole issue.

Monday morning before anyone else is awake, I'm out of the house. Then in harmony class, Miss Ziegler lets me know that I am not to worry. "Miss Welker sent a message to you through me that the money for the lessons will be set-aside whenever you manage to come for them." Even though it's good to hear that, I'm sure it'll be the beginning of difficult times ahead. No matter what, it shows me that you can never know how things are going to turn out. And that's for sure!

*Pennsylvania College for Women now Chatham University

Chapter Twenty-two

A FAMILY SCRAPBOOK
PHOTOGRAPHS

September 12, 1940
Wedding of Elaine Schiffman and Hugo Lowe
[pictured left to right]
Rabbi "Grandpa" Schiffman; Little Sister Barbara Lea;
"The Author", Shirley Ruth Schiffman; "Grandma" Schiffman;
Aunt Elaine and Uncle Hugo ; "Mother" Elizabeth Karpilow Schiffman;
"Uncle Sam" & "Father" Irving Schiffman

**My
Parents**

Elizabeth

Imre

Mother and father before meeting
and after they were married.

Irving Schiffman

Elizabeth Karpilow Schiffman

Elaine "Munie, Elonka"
Schiffman

My
Father's
Family

The
Schiffman's

Samuel "Shonyee,Shmuel"
Schiffman

Irving
"Imre, Avrahm, Itzick"
Schiffman

Frank & Mary "Ephraim
& Miriam" Schiffman

Grandpa & Irving

The Rabbi & his sons: Sibling Rivalry

Grandpa & Sam

Rabbi Frank Schiffman

Sam's Fur Store

The Brothers, Sam & Irving

Cousin Marilyn Bass,
Bubbie & Mayme Karpilow
Bass and Uncle Louis Bass
at Shirley's wedding.

My Mother's
Family:

The Karpilows
&
The Levitins

My mother's mother,
my bubbie:
Rose Levitin Karpilow

Four Cousins:
Shirley & Barbara with
Sammy & Marilyn Bass

Betty Levitin Levy & her father,
Abe Levitin, my Bubbie's brother
& owner of Belmar
Moving & Storage Co.

Elizabeth, Shirley
& Barbara.

Our
Family

Irving, Elizabeth,
Shirley & Barbara.

Shirley & Barbara.

Irving & Daughters
after mother dies.

Irving & Thelma,
his second wife.

Thelma Friedman Schiffman's Family

Thelma's brother, Irving Friedman & his wife:
Yvette Walters Friedman at
Shirley's thirteenth birthday party.

My Young Friends

Leona
Podolsky

Helen
Patricia
Goldberg

Milton
Wolf

Marlene Goppman
&
Shirley at a picnic

Shirley's thirteenth birthday party

Confirmation Class - June 1949

Backyard Food Fest with Birthday Banana Cake

Chapter Twenty-three

FROM THE FAMILY TABLE
SELECTED RECIPES
1937 TO 2010

This collection of recipes represents only a few of the dozens of food memories scribbled on the backs of envelopes, at the bottom of letters, and often at the top of the gas bill. They are treasures of taste, texture, and smell that are forever with me. The idea of a steaming pot of fresh vegetable soup or golden chicken broth with fluffy matzoh balls and carrots or the heavenly odor of cabbage, onions, and noodles all evoke a lifetime of on-the-spot home cooking, trying out recipes, and above all sharing food with family and friends.

After seventy plus years of watching every Jewish mother and grandmother I ever knew prepare and cook, I have come to rely on my own recollections of our family table including a pinch of this and a slice of that along with perhaps those grapes and pears left over in the refrigerator. And more often than not, a splash of Harvey's Bristol Cream, Mogen David Malaga, or Cabernet Sauvignon and exotic seasonings have spiced up my own recipes.

I thank the family cooks and friends who inspired me with their special confections and gustatory presentations. Their efforts live on through the recipes. These are tried and true methods with the freshest and highest quality ingredients—all taste tested by anyone passing through our kitchens. Most of all, I guarantee for those who follow recipes to the last teaspoon or exact sprinkle of salt, nothing has been left out!

Here then is a celebration of life experienced through our family table. Enjoy!

Shirley Barasch and Family

APPLESAUCE

When I let my husband sample the still warm applesauce and ask him if it needs anything, he always says, "It needs a crust." That is really the secret of my lip-smacking, finger-licking apple delight. It tastes just like apple pie without the crust! My attempts at rolling and achieving the crust of a pie are always a disaster. So for what it is worth, here is the filling. You can add the crust. (The apples, of course, do not get cooked until they are in the crust! The flavorings remain the same.)

INGREDIENTS
- 30+ apples (use a mix of different apples but no mushy texture, *please*!) I prefer firm Jonathan/HoneyCrisp/Pink Lady or Jonagold apples.
- lemon juice
- 1 t vanilla
- 11/2 T cinnamon + at least two whole cinnamon sticks
- small sliver or piece of crystallized ginger
- a little dash of salt
- 1/4 C brown sugar (Stevia or Splenda brand)

DIRECTIONS
Wash apples thoroughly. Peel but throw a few of skins in bottom of pot. Quarter and cut apples into medium and smaller chunks. Sprinkle apples with lemon juice to keep from discoloring and for flavor. Add one cup of water to apples and cover. Put on low heat and bring to simmer. Apples will make a lot of juice.

While simmering, add vanilla, cinnamon, ginger, salt, and granulated sugar or Splenda/Stevia (you may add more to taste). Stir and mash apples with potato masher if you want a smoother sauce. Taste and add more of whatever flavor it needs, including lemon. Remove the cinnamon sticks after applesauce cools. Store in glass jar or bowl in refrigerator (freeze in safe plastic or baggie).

This recipe makes a large amount so there is enough for freezing. This applesauce freezes wonderfully and is a great side dish for any dinner or holiday.

BANANA CAKE

By far our favorite family birthday cake has always been and still is banana cake. Thelma Friedman Schiffman's recipe practically does itself. Finished off with chocolate fudge frosting of your choice makes it so heavenly.

INGREDIENTS
- ½ C shortening
- 1½ C sugar
- ½ t baking powder
- ½ t baking soda
- 2 C flour
- Pinch salt
- ½ C sour milk (You can sour milk with ½ T lemon juice or vinegar to ½ C milk.)
- 1 t vanilla
- 3 ripe, mashed bananas
- ¼ C each, raisins and nuts (optional)

DIRECTIONS
Cream together shortening and sugar. Mix all dry ingredients together. Mix sour milk and vanilla thoroughly.

With electric mixer, alternate mixing dry and liquid ingredients into shortening mixture. Add bananas last; blend thoroughly. Pour into lightly greased and floured pan (11x13). Add nuts and raisins, carefully folding in if using. Tap pan gently on counter to remove air bubbles.

Bake for 40 minutes in 350 degree oven. (Test with tooth pick for doneness.)

Frost with chocolate icing of your choice while cake is still slightly warm.

Don't forget to save some icing for licking off the spoon!

BRISKET—THREE WAYS

This wonderful cut of meat is juicy and tender, makes great gravy and satisfies everyone's craving for soul food. The three versions are from Nanny Alice Goldberg Barasch, Aunt Alice Kronek Barasch and Shirley Schiffman Barasch. All three styles use the same basic ingredients but add a unique touch with different seasonings.

HELPFUL TIPS
- Choose a leaner whole brisket (double and single in one large piece) and have the butcher trim excess fat off the double end. A single cut requires no trimming.
- A single cut is adequate for four to five people; buy a whole brisket for large gatherings.
- Choice graded meat cooks up very tender and is tasty.
- Use a large heavy cast iron pan or stainless steel roaster with a good lid.
- Preheat the oven to 425 degrees to sear and brown the meat.
- Prepare your vegetables before you begin.

INGREDIENTS (basic for all three versions)
- 9–12+ lbs whole brisket with nice single portion/excess fat trimmed off
- 2 large sweet onions, sliced in small chunks
- 4–6 carrots cut in 3–4 inch slices
- 3 cloves chopped garlic
- 2 stalks of celery sliced in 1-inch pieces
- ½ red pepper cut in strips
- 1 C mushroom halves (optional)
- 3 large potatoes, washed but unpeeled, quartered
- 1t each salt and pepper
- 1T paprika
- ½+C ketchup

DIRECTIONS FOR ALL 3 VERSIONS

Sear both sides of meat in 425-degree oven (If needed, add 2 T oil to pot). Coat top side of meat with ½ C of ketchup. Add enough water to cover brisket ½ way up. Spread vegetables over top and around meat in pan; sprinkle seasonings on top.

Reduce temperature to 375 degrees; cook uncovered for 40–60 minutes till ready for slicing. (See next section.) Baste meat during cooking; if water cooks down add more, along with ketchup.

SLICING THE MEAT (an important step in cooking brisket!)

When you can barely put a fork through the center of meat, remove from pan; place on wooden or plastic board. Briskets are long in shape; the grain runs from the thick end to the small point. You must cut across the short width of a brisket, not the long side. Use meat fork to hold meat steady as you slice. Use a very sharp knife (electric preferred) holding knife at slight angle. Do not cut straight down. You will see that the grain of the meat looks like small puzzle pieces as you cut. Slices should be medium or thinner, not thick. Return meat to gravy. Cover pot with tight lid. Finish cooking at 325 degrees using one or combination of three versions below.

NANNY's VERSION 1

After brisket is sliced and in gravy, add potatoes on top; sprinkle with paprika. Taste and re-season (adding more of any original seasonings) to your taste. Cover pot and finish cooking until tender and juicy at 325 degrees. Remove lid of pot towards end if you want potatoes to be crisper.

ALICE's VERSION 2

After searing meat, add seasonings/vegetables *plus* pour a can/ bottle of light beer over brisket. Add a little more ketchup to top of meat and a pinch of sugar to sweeten gravy*.

Spread a package of Lipton onion soup mix over top of meat. (*Optional: adds intense flavor/salt*).

Baste brisket with gravy until ready for slicing as in original directions. Finish cooking as in version 1.

*Splenda or Stevia may be used to sweeten gravy if needed (Stevia is sweeter! Use less).

SHIRLEY's VERSION 3

Although I have enjoyed the addition of beer, I tried 1+ cups of wine (red or white) instead and found it wonderful. (I do not use the onion soup—too much salt).

Sometimes I add slices of pear/red grapes or even a sliced apple. Fruit does wonders for gravy!

Finish as in other versions.

All three versions use the potatoes, but you can prepare kasha and bow ties, mashed potatoes, or rice as side dishes instead.

There is nothing like a leftover hot brisket sandwich with lots of gravy! I always try to use a larger brisket so that there will be enough for a second day as well as some to go into the freezer.

CABBAGE and NOODLES

This is a satisfying dish from many different cultures. My husband starts salivating when he sees me slicing the cabbage. This recipe is a combination of my husband's mother's (Nanny Alice Goldberg Barasch) and my grandmother's (Miriam Hofstadter Schiffman)—Russian and Hungarian with perhaps a little Rumanian thrown in.

HELPFUL TIPS
- Choose firm, medium or large size head of cabbage, depending on how much you want to prepare. Trim off outside leaves. Wash off cabbage thoroughly. Cut in half for slicing.
- Slice so that the strips of cabbage are narrow and longer. Save the chopped little pieces for the bottom of the pan.
- Sauté strips of at least two large, sweet Vidalia onions with three chopped garlic cloves in a small amount of olive oil (although many cooks prefer butter, I avoid the extra fat and calories! It tastes just as flavorful.).
- Use a very large and deep cast iron frying pan or stainless steel pot for the cabbage; have a lid that fits over piled-up cabbage.
- Cabbage, onions & garlic are a strong combination. You can cook this dish two to three days ahead of serving in order to air out the kitchen. Store in glass, not in plastic! It is better once the flavors have melded. Warm on top of stove or in low heat oven so noodles do not get mushy.

INGREDIENTS
- 1 medium to large cabbage head, sliced in half and then into strips
- 2–3 onions sliced into strips
- 3–4 cloves peeled garlic, chopped very fine
- 1-pound package of medium wide noodles boiled and drained
- Oil, enough olive or vegetable oil to sauté onions/garlic
- 2 C+ water to steam and soften/cook cabbage
- Lemon pepper, white pepper, kosher salt, and paprika to taste (for browning)

DIRECTIONS

Sauté onions/garlic in oil till golden brown. (Use paprika to help with browning process. Set aside in bowl.)

Put cabbage strips in large frying pan—an iron skillet works best. Add at least 2 cups of water to steam and allow to soften quite a bit. Stir and cook cabbage until at least three-quarters done but not completely cooked.

While cabbage is cooking, boil noodles; drain. (Do not salt water; rinse noodles with cool water.) When cabbage is almost cooked, add onion mixture to cabbage and mix thoroughly. Season to taste. Add noodles and mix again.

Let sit so noodles can absorb the seasoning. Refrigerate if not using immediately.

A wonderful dish to serve with fish or your own favorite entrée.

CHICKEN PAPRIKASH

"I finally got it down on paper," Anne Beetem Barasch (my daughter-in-law, son Larry's wife) explained. She had carefully watched Uncle Sam Schiffman cooking the paprikash, always trying to duplicate his mother's (Grandma's) cooking. This recipe is Anne's transcription of Uncle Sam's version of Grandma's Chicken Paprikash. (I discovered part of Grandma's ingredients on a piece of paper written next to her dumpling recipe: she browned the chicken using the einbrendt—also known as a roux—with lots of onions and paprika. She also added ¼ t sugar to the tomato broth and used fresh garlic.) Either way, it is delicious. (This recipe works with veal or beef, too, according to your tastes.)

INGREDIENTS
- 2 lbs. skinned chicken thighs
- Oil—vegetable, enough for browning
- 1 onion, finely chopped
- 1 carrot, finely grated
- sprigs of parsley, finely chopped
- 12-oz. can of tomato sauce + 1/4 t sugar (opt)
- 1 tsp each salt, pepper, garlic powder, paprika
- 1 C orzo noodles (uncooked) or dumplings (optional)

DIRECTIONS
In large cooking pot brown cleaned and skinned chicken in vegetable oil [enough to coat the bottom of pot) over medium heat (or in einbrendt mixed with lots of onions and 2T flour/paprika. See Grandma's einbrendt recipe.) Remove chicken from pot when browned on all sides. Drain on paper towels.

Add a little more oil to pot and sauté extra onions, chopped garlic, and carrot. Add parsley, salt, pepper, paprika, and garlic powder while sautéing. Pour in the tomato sauce and sugar. Add the chicken and enough water to cover. Stir. At this point, you can add another 1/2 t each salt and pepper plus 1T paprika. (If the chicken is kosher, you may not need any more salt. Taste.).

Cover with lid. Simmer on med-low heat for 2 hours. Stir to make sure nothing sticks to bottom of pot. After 2 hours, take the chicken out of pot. Put on plate till cool enough to handle. Take the cooled chicken and pull it off the bone in chunks. Don't shred it! Place the chicken back in the thickened broth. Fold in gently.

Optional from Anne: "After removing the chicken to cool, add a cup of uncooked orzo noodles to broth to thicken it or make dumplings to add before serving. My family prefers the orzo. Stir the orzo often so it doesn't stick to the bottom. Taste the broth and adjust seasonings. It always needs more paprika, if you ask me. Let the noodles cook for about 15 min."

Bring the chicken back up to temperature and serve with bread. Yum!

CHICKEN SOUP

Whatever the prescription, the reputation of a steaming hot bowl of chicken soup has no equal as a cure for the common cold. Even inhaling the vapors is celebrated in myth. Contests continually declare the greatest chicken soup. Heads are crowned with queen or king of chicken soup making. Cooks come to the process of that special broth often through a variety of shared recipes. I thank every member of my family back several generations for the recipe that follows with, of course, my own special added touches. I wear my crown with pride!

HELPFUL TIPS

- DO NOT USE FROZEN CHICKEN! The flavor is not the same.
- Avoid chickens with additives or hormones. Kosher chickens are the best choice.
- Have the butcher remove all excess fat and skin as much as possible.
- Include chicken neck and backs with skin/fat removed. *Wash chicken thoroughly.*
- Remove all pinfeathers and skin from wings as much as possible.
- Do not skimp on chicken or fresh vegetables. Organic carrots are sweeter.
- A bigger pot is better than going for less soup. The broth freezes well and is a welcome source of comfort when a cold strikes!
- *Use only glass containers* to store *cooled* chicken soup in the refrigerator. Plastic has a tendency to sour the broth.
- *Do not* store chicken soup with noodles. Even one noodle will sour soup.
- Separate the chicken from the broth before storing. Keep the carrots in broth.
- Save the onions, parsnip, celery, etc., squeezing out the extra broth and pressing through a strainer or sieve to get every ounce of vitamins possible. Use that strained broth for other dishes *or* drink it on the spot!
- Use a heavy stainless steel or iron pot. *No aluminum or Teflon!*

INGREDIENTS (for at least 8–10 quarts of soup; feeds 14–16 a big bowl!)

- 1 whole kosher chicken (quartered with back and neck) skinned/fat trimmed
- extra whole legs, and 1 extra large breast with bones in—all skinned
- large turkey leg skinned
- 3–5 lb bag organic carrots, scraped, washed, and cut in thirds or halves
- 1/2 red pepper left whole
- 2 large Vidalia or Spanish onions peeled and scored but not cut up
- 3–4 large, fresh celery stalks, cleaned and cut in thirds. (Add celery hearts, too)
- 2 medium or 1 very large parsnip(s), scraped and cut in half.
- large, ripe, softer tomato cut 1/2 way through but not in pieces
- large bunch of flat-leaf parsley washed (in net or tied with cooking string)
- 4 cloves of fresh garlic, scored
- kosher salt and _white_ pepper to taste

(On occasion I have also used fresh dill in the soup. It adds a very unique flavor.)

DIRECTIONS

Place washed chicken in heavy pot; just barely cover with fresh water. Bring to boil and cook until foam rises to top. Quickly dump chicken and water into cleaned sink and rinse immediately with cold water. Wash pot.

Place chicken with fresh cold water covering it plus 1/4 more water in pot. Place on high heat. Add vegetables (except carrots) in water along with seasoning. There should be enough water to completely cover ingredients plus a little more. Bring to rolling boil. Add seasonings. Reduce heat and place lid on pot. Simmer for at least 2 hours.

If soup boils down, add small amounts of water. Taste to adjust seasonings. From time to time check pot to make sure enough water covers chicken. Taste again and adjust seasonings. When soup chicken is fork tender and broth tastes right, add carrots.

Cover pot. Simmer 10–15 minutes. Turn off heat and let carrots finish cooking in the hot broth. The carrots will retain their texture instead of being mushy. Allow soup to cool enough to handle pot, chicken, and broth.

Soup will be golden, clear and smell wonderful.

STRAINING SOUP.

Straining soup is work-intensive and requires patience. Place a large colander inside a larger heat proof Pyrex. You will need 2+ bowls! For this amount of soup, large mixing bowls/heat proof glass roasters will work. Do not use plastic!

Have a large baking dish (11x13 or roasting pan lined with foil) ready for chicken. Carefully remove chicken (using tongs) to pan. It may fall apart, so use slotted spoon to rescue pieces from broth. Place all carrots to side of pan.

De-bone chicken/turkey leg when cool. (Try to discard gristle/large bones as you go.) Place vegetables in a separate bowl as you work. They will be for the intense broth.

Remove parsley. Squeeze juice out over vegetables. Discard parsley.

Slowly pour soup through colander/strainer into larger bowl. Distribute carrots in saved soup; cool completely before covering and refrigerating. Squeeze juice from other vegetables, pressing through colander/strainer into a smaller bowl. Or save vegetables whole for those who love them with their soup.

Babies can enjoy the purée of vegetables and soup early on. If you mix the purréd vegetables with regular soup, the broth will be cloudy. It will still be delicious! Serve with fine noodles, matzoh balls, or dumplings.

Your house will have an intense fragrance and everyone will be salivating for a bowl. Be sure to save broth for the freezer, adding some of the de-boned chicken. Chicken from soup makes wonderful sandwiches, chicken salad, or a base for spaghetti sauce. You can also put chicken pieces into an airtight freezer bag with some gravy made from chicken broth and the einbrendt. It is an instant home-cooked dinner whenever! Smaller amounts of soup require the same process and same effort. Go for the big pot!

CHOLENT

Just reading my sister Barbara Schiffman Samet's cholent recipe brought back the smell of my grandma's kitchen as she prepared it on Thursday getting ready for our Saturday lunch or dinner after sundown. The richness of the beans mixed with duck or chicken schmaltz (rendered fat), slices of brisket, short ribs—nice and fatty—along with stuffed kishke (stuffed entrails) and hearty barley (cooking all night in the oven) left no one hungry, that was for sure! As our cousin Deanna Lowe Sable said about her memory of the cholent, "Grandma's was soft, mushy, and tasty because it had lots of cholesterol in it!" I have long since given up the extra calories and fat. Barbara's recipe substitutes hot dogs for kishke and limits the fat (somewhat) to the short ribs and brisket. My grandma used a heavy roaster for all her oven cooking. Let me tell you, I remember well scrubbing those pots for Grandma's inspection. My sister uses a heavy foil throwaway pan! Saves a lot of fingernails.

INGREDIENTS
- 2 C red kidney beans soaked overnight (rinse/pick over/remove any skins)
- 1 large onion, chopped
- 2–3 cloves garlic, chopped fine
- 4–5 lb brisket (trim only heavy fat off)
- 12–15 kosher hot dogs
- 3–5 short ribs and beef bones if available
- 1 C pearl barley, rinsed
- powdered beef broth (optional), salt, pepper, Hungarian paprika
- large throwaway foil pan

DIRECTIONS
Preheat oven to 400 degrees. Prepare beans and barley. Put in foil pan. Sauté onions and garlic in frying pan; add to foil pan. Mix thoroughly. Cover with water and bring to boil in oven.

Add bones and whole short ribs to liquid. Make sure you have it all covered with water! Reduce heat to 325-350 and cook for

10–15 hours (overnight). Get up during the night to make sure there is enough water in pan.

In the morning, add brisket and cook for 3–4 hours more. Add other seasonings to taste. Keep covered with water.

One hour before you serve, skim off excess fat. Add hot dogs, pushing them under the beans and meat. Make sure they are covered with beans and meat.

Slice the brisket before serving. Taste from pot to re-season.

Be prepared for lots of slurping and mmming sounds.

GRANDMA'S DUMPLINGS

Grandma always made dumplings to go with her paprikash. Her recipe is very simple and easy to make. (Other dumpling recipes use baking powder or oil, add parsley, and require kneading.)

I remember my grandma showing me how to simply take the edge of a spoon/fork with a little of the finished dough and with a flick of my fingernail drop it into boiling water. One, two, three— no fuss—no muss. Make them as large or small as you like. Small pieces are called spaetzle! They take less time to cook.

INGREDIENTS
- 1/2 lb flour in large bowl
- 2 beaten eggs with a little water
- 1/2 t salt and pepper to taste
- 1 t sugar
- water or oil if needed

DIRECTIONS

Mix eggs with salt, pepper, and sugar. Make a well in center of flour and add egg mixture. Mix with large wooden spoon till not too loose or hard. Add water or a little oil if needed to make dough easier to handle.

Bring large pot of water to rolling boil. Drop dough from edge of spoon/fork into boiling water. When they float to top, taste one for doneness. Remove with slotted spoon to strainer or colander. Work quickly. Rinse all at once in cold water.

Serve with paprikash or veal stew or in soup.

FAT-FREE HONEY CAKE

Among my favorite holidays is Rosh Hashanah—the Jewish New Year! Coming just when the finish of summer is edged out by a sudden shift of hot wind to an early fall chill at night, it signals the arrival of a crunchy crop of apples, the smell of fresh chicken soup and brisket in the kitchen, and the sticky delight of honey cake coming out of the oven. Where Thelma Friedman Schiffman got this wonderful recipe is not clear. It is, however, with or without walnuts the best finger-lickin' treat for the new moon—which always coincides with Rosh Hashanah...literally the head of the year!

HELPFUL TIPS
- Use a deeper 11x13 pan for even baking rather than loaf pans.
- Line the pan with heavy duty foil...smooth it out over sides.
- Let cake cool completely before lifting out of pan.
- Use a deep pot for cooking honey as the baking soda/coffee will foam up!

INGREDIENTS
- 1-lb jar honey
- 2 t baking soda
- 1 C black coffee—hot
- 3 eggs
- 1 C sugar
- 3 C flour
- 1 t cinamon
- Several walnut halves (optional)

DIRECTIONS
In a large deep pot, heat honey to boiling. Add baking soda and then hot, black, strong coffee. Let cool.

Beat eggs, adding sugar gradually to cream together. Mix flour and cinnamon. Then alternately pour flour and egg mixture into cooled honey liquid. Mix thoroughly (use handheld electric mixer) after each addition.

Pour batter into foil lined pan. Place walnut halves over top of batter (optional). Tap pan on counter to remove air bubbles. Bake in preheated oven (300 degrees) for 50–55 minutes. Test center of cake with a toothpick to ensure cake is baked through. However, cake will finish baking out of oven in the foil-lined pan just from its own heat.

This cake guarantees a sweet year!

GEFILTE FISH©

Miriam Barasch Fleming's adaptation of a family recipe
presented in her exact words.

This recipe is adapted from the recipe of my aunt Barbara Schiffman Samet, who tells me her mother (my grandmother) gave it to her on her deathbed. My grandmother got it from her mother-in-law and so on and so forth back several generations in a small village in Hungary. With my aunt's permission, I am giving it to you. This recipe is a "sweet" style Gefilte Fish. I have modified it from the original proportions, which serve 100, to this recipe for approximately twenty 3-inch diameter balls, which serve a course for 10–15 people. I have also changed the recipe to include amounts of ingredients and cooking times instead of that which my aunt gave me including such instructions as "add all seasoning to taste; cook until smells done; and how many eggs depends on how wet the fish is." That being said, as with all good family cooking, much of the success of this recipe will depend on you making it your own by making it sweeter or more savory, heavier or lighter to the tastes of your family. Good luck and have fun! I hope this recipe will become a tradition in your family the way it is in mine!

Bragging rights from Miriam's mother and Elizabeth Samet's Aunt, Shirley Barasch: Miriam (Mimmi to her parents) Fleming used this same recipe two years ago in a cooking class she was teaching in Milwaukee. Miriam is a wonderful cook who trained with Ferdinand Metz at The Heinz Company in Pittsburgh and at The Cornell School of Hotel and Restaurant Management before taking up the law as a second profession. Making this fish from scratch is an art that is not easily duplicated. Therefore, I am including every word and list as she sent it to me. The horseradish sauce, which is a must with the fish, follows. David Winitsky (Barbara's son-in-law, married to daughter Elizabeth) is now the certified Gefilte Fish maker for all the major holidays in their New Jersey family. No, he is not available for Bar Mitzvahs or weddings! But as a first-rate director and writer, David along with Lizzie can whip up a script right along with the fish!

EQUIPMENT LIST
- meat grinder (electric)
- blender
- 12-qt pot
- dry and liquid measuring cups
- vegetable peeler
- measuring spoons
- sharp knives
- slotted spoon
- wooden spoon
- large mixing bowl
- small bowl for cracking eggs into
- large fine mesh strainer
- large glass container for storing finished fish
- 1-qt glass jar with tight-fitting lid for storing horseradish sauce

Stock
The stock will be used to poach the fish balls. Prepare stock first. The skin, heads, and bones will come from the fish, which is filleted for the fish balls. For this recipe size, you may need to ask fishmonger for additional heads/bones/skins for amounts listed below.

Make sure you ask the fishmonger to *remove the eyes from the heads of all fish.*

STOCK INGREDIENTS
- 2 pounds white fish skin bones and heads
- 2 pounds walleye pike fish skin, bones and heads
- 1 medium whole onion (peeled)
- 2½–3 pounds whole carrots (preferably organic), cleaned, peeled, and cut into 4–6" pieces
- 5 ribs celery whole, cleaned
- 2 large cloves fresh garlic peeled
- 2 ½ T salt (I suggest sea salt; if using regular salt, reduce by ½ T.)
- ½ t white pepper
- 4 t sweet paprika
- 1 T garlic powder
- 2/3 C sugar

STOCK DIRECTIONS

Rinse skin, bones, and heads well, removing all blood and membranes from them, paying special attention to eye sockets. Fill large (12-qt) pot 1/3 full with 4 quarts warm water. Add cleaned fish heads, skin, and bones to pot. Add remaining ingredients (pot will be about ½ full).

Bring to boil, stirring to blend ingredients. Adjust seasoning to taste. Stock should be double strength to finished fish balls. Turn off heat while making fish balls. Return to boil before adding balls.

GEFILTE FISH BALLS

Gefilte fish is really just a fish dumpling. How dense the dumpling depends on the amount of eggs. This recipe is for a medium density ball. The fish fillets may be ordered pre-ground from fish store. I prefer to grind the fish with the onion and carrot because it provides a better distribution both for taste and appearance.

INGREDIENTS

- 2 lbs white fish fillets (no skin) rinsed, any bones removed, cut into small 2" pieces
- 2 lbs walleye pike fillets (no skin) rinsed, remove bones, cut into small 2" pieces
- ½ medium onion peeled (cut into wedges if grinding with fish; otherwise, grate finely)
- 1–2 carrots (for color) cut into 1" wedge if grinding with fish; otherwise, grate finely
- 1 T + 1 t garlic powder
- ½ t white pepper
- 1 T + 2 t salt
- ½ cup sugar (Use up to another additional ½ cup sugar for sweet style fish.)
- 4–5 eggs

FISH BALL DIRECTIONS

Grind fish with electric meat grinder alternating fish with piece of onions and carrots to evenly disperse. (If using pre-ground fish, add finely grated carrots/onions until evenly dispersed). Mix in garlic powder, pepper, and sugar. Mix in 1 egg at a time (break into a separate bowl before adding in) until mixture holds together and is light in texture.

To adjust seasoning to taste make small (1/2" diameter) "test balls." Cook in boiling stock. Balls will initially sink. Balls are done for taste testing when they pop up and float. Cool balls in freezer or refrigerator before tasting. Place remainder of fish mixture in refrigerator while doing test batches. Once seasoned to taste, form approximately 2½–3" diameter balls using hands moistened with water. Set aside in refrigerator while you bring stock to boil.

Bring stock to boil. Add fish balls to boiling stock. Pot will be ¾ full. Once stock returns to full boil, cook 30 minutes in covered pot/ lid ¼ open. Reduce heat to medium simmer. Cook additional 45 minutes (total cooking time of 1 ½ hours.) Fish will be "cooked" sooner, but in order for the stock to penetrate the entire fish ball, it needs to cook the longer time period. For very large balls (3½–5 inches in diameter), cook 2 hours total.

Cool in pot until cool enough to handle (approximately 2 hours). Remove carrots and fish balls from pot. Balls may stick together; break apart gently. Rinse fish and carrots lightly to remove any debris from stock. Place in large deep glass container. (Do not use plastic!) Strain stock through fine mesh strainer over fish balls and carrots.

Refrigerate until cold (overnight). Serve cold with stock juice, carrots, and horseradish sauce. Stock may gel into light aspic consistency. If so, serve with some of the aspic, which will liquefy as you serve and eat.

The best part of having the fish was the inevitable finding of the bone that escaped my aunt Barbara's eagle eye and ended up almost always in my mother Shirley's fish ball! Even so, my mother always exclaimed that, "It was the best fish Aunt Barbara ever made." This dish was center stage for Rosh Hashanah (the Jewish New Year) and Passover. However, we all enjoyed it more when we could dip fresh challah into the golden juice—especially flavored with a little horseradish sauce.

HORSERADISH SAUCE

How hot the horseradish turns out to be is purely a factor of the radish and mostly out of control of the cook. Make sure you use fresh radish for the best heat potential. Makes approximately 1 quart.

HORSERADISH SAUCE INGREDIENTS
- 1 large peeled horseradish root
- 1 can whole Beets including juice (more as needed). Cut beets into smaller pieces.
- 1 C sugar (more as needed, approximately ½ C–2 C ground radish root)

HORSERADISH SAUCE DIRECTIONS
Grind horseradish using meat grinder (completely cleaned from fish preparation). Be prepared, this process can be very harsh on the eyes, much worse than cutting onions.

In batches combine beets including juice with ½ C sugar and 2 C ground horseradish in blender. Reserve rest of radish for next step. Strain juice from the blended mixture and retain separately. Combine strained beet juice with 2 additional C ground horseradish and additional ½ C sugar. Repeat until all horseradish is combined (including first strained batch) using more beets (blended) and sugar as needed, depending on how hot the radish is.

Immediately transfer to glass jar; close lid tightly. (This helps retain the radish heat.) Chill. Serve cold with Gefilte Fish.

©Copyright 2005 Miriam Barasch

Note from Shirley Barasch: My grandmother, Mary Hofstadter Schiffman, frequently made what she called "falseh fish" when regular fish was too expensive or out of season. She used chicken mixed with veal, substituting chicken backs, necks, etc., and veal bones for the stock and balls. The rest of the ingredients were almost identical. I don't remember anyone enjoying it as much as the real Gefilte Fish, which beats the supermarket fish loaf, which is frozen or in a jar, by more than a mile. If you undertake the extensive effort required to really make Gefilte Fish from scratch, make sure you have plenty of fresh challah to dip into the luscious juice. It is worth every aching muscle in your back and the burning eyes and bleeding knuckles from the horseradish.

Remember! Do not use plastic containers, glass only!

KASHA VARNISHKAS or KASHA AND BOW TIES

This hearty combination of buckwheat kernels, onions, garlic, salt, pepper and paprika never fails to enhance any main dish from beef to chicken! It was among the favorite dishes my mother-in-law (Nanny Alice Goldberg Barasch) served her family. As with almost all ethnic foods, the addition of lots of garlic and onions is vital to the satisfying odor and flavor. In today's kitchen you will fulfill the requirement of whole grains with kasha but even more if you use whole wheat bow ties.

HELPFUL TIPS
- Cook up lots of onions and garlic in a small amount of oil first.
- Make sure you brown the kasha thoroughly using more oil and paprika, but do not totally dry it out!
- Be careful when adding water to kasha, as you can easily burn yourself with splatters!

INGREDIENTS
- ½ box buckwheat kasha, fine, medium, or coarse (I use Wolff's brand.)
- egg, beaten
- 2 large onions
- cloves garlic, chopped
- 2½ cups of boiling water
- salt, pepper, etc., as you like
- ½ pkg bow tie noodles, cooked according to directions

DIRECTIONS
Cook finely diced onions in just enough oil; combine with garlic. Brown and set aside in another bowl (it will be added to dish later).

Brown dried kasha directly out of box using small amount of oil in same pan until almost dry. Mix in beaten egg. When browned, add boiling water fast over kasha. Add seasonings to liquid before it all cooks down. Stir! Do not let kasha stick to pan.

Cover and steam over lowest flame until all liquid is absorbed. Taste for balance of seasoning, then add all the onions and garlic and mix thoroughly.

Add bow ties, mix, and allow to set. Enjoy with or without gravy!

P.S.: You can substitute tasty leftover chicken broth for some of the water.

PICKLED CUCUMBERS

What a wonderful crunchy sweet/sour condiment! It is especially tasty when the summer crop of cucumbers is at its height. I don't know where Thelma, my stepmother, got the recipe, but both my sister and I have adapted it to our own tastes. Thelma was very sure that her system gave the best results, and I am inclined to agree. Here it is.

HELPFUL TIPS
- Choose firm, thin cucumbers and a large sweet onion (Spanish/ Vidalia).
- Avoid reactive pans or containers; use glass (Ball jars), sparkling clean!
- Splenda/Stevia avoids the extra sugar and calories.
- The wax paper avoids contact of acid with metal lid; it seals well, too.
- Squeezing the water out of the pickles helps them absorb the flavors.

INGREDIENTS
- 4–8 firm dark green cucumbers; thinner ones are not mushy
- large, sweet onion cut in very thin slices and set aside
- clove of garlic peeled and scored
- equal parts of cider vinegar (or apple), water, and then sugar to taste (or Splenda)
- salt, pepper, lots of paprika

DIRECTIONS
Wash and peel cucumbers; slice thin, but not paper thin. Put in a large glass bowl; sprinkle thoroughly with salt. Place a heavy plate directly on top of cucumbers so it presses down on them. Put in refrigerator overnight.

In morning, turn bowl upside down over sink holding on to plate to drain water. In a large clean wide mouthed jar, layer onions with cucumbers, sprinkling pepper, salt, and paprika over each layer. Go light on seasoning; you can always add more. Throw in the garlic clove. Have a tight-fitting lid for jar plus wax paper.

In another large glass container, with a lid, mix the vinegar, water, and seasonings including paprika and sugar. Make sure lid is tight! Shake well. Taste the liquid brine for a balance of sweet and sour and tart.

Pour liquid over the cucumbers in the other jar. Place wax paper over jar opening and seal with lid, screwing on tightly. Shake jar to mix and refrigerate for several hours. You can test the flavor and doneness after 1–2 hours. The longer it marinates, the better the pickles.

What a delicious accompaniment for meat and salads or as a salad dressing!

QUICK FILET OF BEEF, CHICKEN, VEAL WITH SPECIAL SAUCE USING AN EINBRENDT

This recipe takes off from the basic brisket sauce (which can be prepared and even frozen days in advance) to make a wonderful company dinner using slices of raw steak, chicken, or veal that is cooked quickly and served with fork tender vegetables, fruit, and gravy right out of the pan on the stove onto each plate.

HELPFUL TIPS

- Use a heavy but not too deep frying pan, as you need to put the meat in the bubbling sauce and cook it quickly.
- Prepare all the vegetables before beginning.
- Wash and pat dry thoroughly cleaned prepared meat, chicken, etc
- Refrigerate on covered flat dish or pan.
- Tasting the sauce is vital to the finished product. Let your lips/ tongue guide you!
- My grandma's einbrendt is a wonderful prelude to rich and thick gravy for all kinds of dishes like Chicken Paprikash and Veal Stew. Although for this dish, it is worth the extra time it takes.
- Always use small amounts of flour to begin till you judge the thickness of sauce.
- Always mix the flour with a small amount of water to strain through to the sauce.
- Use a long arm potholder and a flexible set of tongs for browning meat.

INGREDIENTS: BASIC SAUCE RECIPE (for a large gathering)

- 3–4 whole large sweet onions (Spanish/Vidalia) cut in longer strips
- 3–4 cloves garlic diced
- 2 whole peppers (red and green) cut in longer strips
- 2 celery stalks cut in small slices
- 1 C sliced mushrooms or whole button mushrooms (optional)
- ¼ C tomato sauce (or ketchup if preferred)

- 1–2 C wine (red for beef; white for chicken) to taste/added last
- pinch sugar (Splenda/Stevia if desired) to balance the wine flavor
- salt, lemon pepper, small piece of crystallized ginger, Zahatar, paprika
- red seedless grapes and slices of pear and apple (optional but wonderful for flavor)
- oil—olive or vegetable
- water
- ¼ C flour
- einbrendt

DIRECTIONS FOR SAUCE

Heat oil in pan and sauté onions and garlic first till lightly browned. Put in bowl. Sauté celery & peppers using more oil if needed in same pan. Add enough water to just cover vegetables; bring to simmer. Add tomato sauce, stir, and simmer; then, add the onions to sauce. Add salt, etc., to simmering sauce and allow to cook down. Add water as needed to keep from burning; add mushrooms; cook down again. Taste and fix seasonings if needed.

Add 1 C wine and stir to mix. Simmer and add pinch of sugar. Add 1 C water; cover, and simmer on low heat. Your pan should have at least 3–4 inches of liquid including vegetables and wine. If you feel you need more seasoning, add it; save some wine to add sparingly if the flavor needs it, or to toast yourself while cooking!

Throw in the fruit; stir gently and cover and set aside. Fruit will cook in hot sauce.

GRANDMA'S EINBRENDT (for small amount of quick thickening and flavoring)

- 1+ onions, chopped fine (onion can be omitted, but it's a plus in einbrendt)
- 2 + T all-purpose flour (enough to make a paste)
- ¼ C oil, enough to cover bottom of small frying pan
- salt and pepper to taste

DIRECTIONS

If using onions: Sauté onions first until clarified in oil, then add flour, salt, and pepper, stirring constantly to blend in. Scrape bottom of pan to keep from burning. A wooden spoon works best. Set aside in bowl.

DIRECTIONS FOR COOKING MEAT/CHICKEN/VEAL

Take the meat /chicken out of refrigerator and allow to come to room temperature. Dry with paper towels.

Dip each piece of meat in flour shaking excess off. Using same pan, add oil to cover bottom of pan; brown each piece on both sides. When browned, drain on paper towels; set aside on plate. Make sure chicken (if using) juices run clear after browning!

Bring sauce back to a simmer. Using strainer, pour einbrendt mix into simmering sauce; stir constantly to blend. Taste/adjust seasonings or amount of liquid; bring to rolling boil to cook meat. Take each piece of meat and lower carefully into sauce; cook to desired doneness. Check for doneness by cutting slightly into thickest part of meat, etc.

Sauce will thicken as it cooks. Serve straight out of pan onto serving platter or onto each plate. Give everyone a choice of fruit with gravy on top. Serve with any of your favorite mashed potatoes, brown rice, or kasha. The gravy can be frozen and reheated with or without meat, chicken, etc.

Company often wants to sop up the gravy and sometimes even drink it!

SLUM GUM

I always knew when money was tight! There were endless bowls of overly thickened stew or soup. I also often served (to our three children) French toast with applesauce or cereal with raisins forming smiling faces to get through the end of the month. One economical dish that turned out to be everyone's favorite was a mixture of macaroni, ground beef or chicken and vegetables baked crisp in the oven. We still serve it and affectionately refer to it as "slum gum."

HELPFUL HINTS
- Do not use too much liquid, it makes the noodles mushy.
- Make sure the vegetables are thoroughly sautéed before adding to cooked noodles.
- Use a large oven proof glass container/Pyrex bowl.
- This is made best in a heavy cast iron skillet, but the Pyrex bowl acts as a server at same time. One less pot to wash!

INGREDIENTS
- 1½ lbs lean ground beef
- 4 stalks celery, chopped fine
- green or red pepper chopped in small pieces
- 4 cloves garlic, diced fine
- large sweet onion, chopped fine
- can tomato soup (Campbell's Cream of Tomato)
- 1 can water—use soup can and get all sauce out of it
  NOTE: When increasing the size of the recipe, use 2 cans soup and water.
  A second can of tomato soup with no added water makes it saucier.
- salt and pepper to taste
- 1 lb. box elbow macaroni cooked al dente

DIRECTIONS

Brown the ground beef in its own fat. Add small amount of oil if needed. Ground meat should be crumbly and browned. Put in lightly greased pyrex.

In same pan, add small amount of oil and cook onions, celery, garlic, and peppers. Do not over brown vegetables; they will cook further in oven. Dump tomato soup over vegetables and stir, gradually adding water; bring to simmer.

Add seasonings and taste. Add more or less of what you like. Add sauce to ground meat and stir to evenly distribute sauce with meat.

Boil elbow macaroni till not quite al dente; drain and rinse. Mix with meat and sauce and finish in oven at 350 degrees until crisp on top and sides.

Serve with applesauce and crunchy bread on the side. Mmmmmm!

THANKSGIVING SPECIALTIES

Thanksgiving turkey is an American tradition that makes it a feast for the eyes as well as the appetite. There are hundreds of methods and approaches to roasting and carving the big bird. But when it comes to stuffing, gravy, and sweet potatoes, nothing in my experience can beat the tasty specialities that my stepmother, Thelma, turned out flawlessly again and again.

STUFFING

HELPFUL TIPS
- Follow the directions exactly for best results.
- Tasting is imperative.
- Although stuffing the bird gives wonderful results, the stuffing tastes as good baked in a separate Pyrex bowl. Saves a lot of oven time!
- Dried challah at least three days old is better than commercial cubed bags of stuffing.
- Wash your hands thoroughly in order to work the stuffing seasoning through.
- Avoid using jarred gravy/mixes. Instead, make your own gravy by buying an extra turkey neck or wing, etc., and following directions below.

INGREDIENTS
- large loaf of challah, dried, at least 3–5 days old
- 2 white potatoes, peeled, boiled, drained, and mashed
- 1 large sweet onion peeled and diced
- 3 stalks celery diced
- 2–3 cloves garlic, diced
- 4 eggs, beaten
- pinch of baking powder and pinch of baking soda
- salt, white pepper, and more garlic powder after you taste the final mixture

DIRECTIONS

Squeeze warm water thoroughly through and out of bread; put in large pot or mixing bowl. Add mashed potatoes to bread. Mix thoroughly with hands.

Sauté onions, celery, garlic till gold but not too brown. When cool enough to handle, add to bread and potato mixture. Blend (using hands) the eggs and seasoning mixture into bread mixture.

Lightly grease a heat/ovenproof dish large enough for mixture and pour in, leaving space in the top of bowl for stuffing to rise (or stuff turkey with mixture leaving enough room in cavity for expansion.).

Bake stuffing in heat proof glass till brown on top and sides at 300-350 degrees.

For stuffed turkey follow directions according to size, etc.

GIBLET GRAVY

When you roast the turkey throw the liver, neck, gizzard (poupick), and any other spare turkey parts into the pan along with enough water on bottom to cook items through. If you are dry roasting/basting the turkey, put all the giblets, etc., into a bowl or pan and roast next to turkey. Use enough water to make it almost a stew. Remove when cooked through. When turkey is done and is resting before being carved, finish the gravy.

DIRECTIONS

Save the drippings from the bottom of the pan in which you roasted the turkey, including any little black tasty parts, and add to giblet mix in pan. Strain into smaller pan and add can of mushrooms with liquid (optional). Cut up cooked liver, gizzard, etc., and return to pan and simmer.

Make an einbrendt (roux) paste with oil and cold water in a glass bowl and strain into simmering gravy liquid. It will thicken as it simmers. (See Grandma's Einbrendt directions).

Taste and season as needed. Serve over turkey and stuffing.

CANDIED SWEET POTATOES

HELPFUL TIPS
- Begin this dish on top of stove in a heavy cast iron skillet.
- Finish the dish in the oven (not microwave) on about 350 degrees.
- Notice the optional added ingredients that give a tasty change to the same dish.

INGREDIENTS
- 4–6 sweet potatoes or yams, quartered
- 1–2 firm, crisp apples peeled, and quartered (sprinkle with lemon juice)
- brown sugar (or Splenda)
- ¼ t vanilla
- margarine

DIRECTIONS

Arrange fruit and potatoes over bottom of heavy iron skillet. Add water to barely cover. Sprinkle brown sugar or Splenda and vanilla and dot with margarine over apples and potatoes.

Bring to boil; reduce heat and simmer till potatoes are fork tender. Finish in preheated oven (350 degrees) until glazed and syrupy. Baste!

SHIRLEY'S OPTIONAL ADDED INGREDIENTS FOR A ZINGY TASTE CHANGE:

Add a pkg raw washed cranberries to simmering liquid with sweet potatoes and apples cooking on top of stove. Add 2–3 pieces of chopped crystallzed ginger. Add a piece of orange zest plus pieces of cut up oranges (no pith). Add ¼ C of orange juice if more liquid is needed. Finish in oven as above.

This optional addition makes the dish like a hot chutney and is a wonderful substitute for the usual cranberry side dish.

VEGETABLE SOUP

My father's second wife, my stepmother, Thelma Friedman Schiffman, was an excellent cook. It was always a great treat for my birthday when she made one of my favorite soups: cabbage or vegetable. I usually had a hard time deciding, but invariably if I chose vegetable, by the end of winter we would also have cabbage. Those soups warmed my tummy as well as my spirits.

MEATLESS VEGETABLE SOUP INGREDIENTS (for a large pot of soup, saving some for the freezer)
Choose only fresh, firm, and unblemished vegetables. Whatever is available during the summer from local farmers is the best bet for hearty soup.

- small box fresh string beans (washed, trimmed, and cut in half)
- large sweet onions, chopped medium sized
- 3–4 stalks celery, sliced down (add celery hearts as well)
- large red potato cut in smaller pieces
- sweet potato or yam cut in medium pieces
- cloves of garlic chopped very fine
- cups of shredded/chopped cabbage
- 1 C+ corn off fresh ears (or use Birdseye flash frozen with no additives)
- 1 C+ fresh peas (or use Birdseye flash frozen with no additives)
- 1 lb+ organic carrots cut in ½ inch slices
- 2–3 large, fresh, ripe tomatoes cut in medium chunks with skin and seeds included
- ½ each green and red pepper cut in small pieces
- box/can salt- & MSG- free tomato puree (Pomi brand is a good choice.)
- just enough fresh cold water to cover all vegetables and soup bones (if using).
- salt, lemon pepper, Mrs. Dash salt-free general seasoning to taste

DIRECTIONS

Bring all ingredients to rolling boil uncovered. Cook at a simmer for 1 hour.

FOR BEEF OR CHICKEN VEGETABLE SOUP

Brown ¾ –1 lb beef cubes or cut up chicken in small amount of oil. Drain thoroughly. Add to soup that has cooked at a simmer for 1 hour. Add beef bones that are washed and patted dry to soup if you want. Simmer in covered pot for an additional 1 hour or until taste is as you like it. Store cooled soup in heat proof Pyrex in refrigerator or prepare for freezer. Let soup sit in refrigerator for 1 day to absorb the full flavors of ingredients.

On occasion I have added broccoli, cauliflower, parsnip, turnip or mushrooms. They, however, are very strong vegetables and can overwhelm the other flavors. The same is true of other kinds of beans, especially lima. When reheating soup, do so as you need it to avoid boiling soup down too much.

This hearty soup makes an entire meal by itself with crusty bread and butter.

ABOUT THE AUTHOR

Professor Emerita Shirley R. Barasch, Ph.D., is a composer, lyricist, singing teacher, published poet/playwright, and teacher-educator. Among her many awards was recognition for her appearance in the Warner Cable Television Award Winning "The Value of Music-Movement in Early Childhood Education." She has received the "Performing Arts Partnership Award" for contributions to the arts; fourteen ASCAP (American Society of Composers, Authors and Publishers) awards; numerous poetry and short fiction prizes; as well as being featured as a Guest Poet of *Taproot Literary Journal.* At Point Park University in Pittsburgh, Pennsylvania, she served as Chair for the Conservatory of Performing Arts; Director of Music and Fine Arts, and as Teacher Educator/Director of Student Teachers. She created the "Starmakers Gala" and the "PAPA Award" for the Conservatory raising money for the Pittsburgh Playhouse and University. She currently lives with her husband Ron in Mt. Lebanon, Pa., teaching singing, composing and writing in her studio while trying hard to keep track of their ten grandchildren.

For more information on the work of Dr. Shirley Barasch see her two Web sites:

MaryShelley.org or **ShirleyBarasch.org**

E-MAIL: sbaraschstudio@verizon.net

The following are available through the author:
DVD *Mary Shelley and Her Frankenstein* **(Live Performance, 2008)**
CD *Alice in Wonderland* **(Live Performance, 1995)**
CD *The Emperor's Nightingale* **(Live Performance, 1986)**
CD *Pages of a Diary* **(Live Performance, 2005)**

Made in the USA
Lexington, KY
23 October 2011